We hope you enjoy *How to Be Baseball Star*!

If this book inspire you, helps you improve your skills, or brings a smile to your face, we'd love to hear about it. Writing a quick **review on Amazon** not only helps us improve but also helps other young football fans discover this book. Your thoughts matter, and they can make a big difference in getting the word out to future stars like you! Thank you for being a part of our team!

Contents

Chapter 1

Operation Awesome Baseball Player

So here you are, future baseball star, ready to begin your journey to greatness! Maybe you've been watching MLB highlights for hours, dreaming of making those amazing plays. Or maybe you're just tired of being the kid who ducks every time the ball comes your way (hey, we've all been there!).

Your baseball glove might be stiff as a board, your throws might look more like adventure missions than strikes, and your batting stance might make your coach scratch their head - but guess what? Every single baseball legend started somewhere, and most of them were probably just as wobbly as you feel right now.

Here's a little secret: Those pro players you watch on TV? They used to miss easy catches, throw balls over fences, and yes, sometimes even run the wrong way around the bases. The difference is they kept trying, kept learning, and kept believing they could get better. And that's exactly what you're about to do!

Fun Facts That'll Blow Your Mind!

- Did you know? Baseballs used to be made with fish eyes in the center!
- Wow Factor: MLB players go through about 900,000 balls per season!
- Mind Blown: A baseball travels faster than a cheetah can run!
- Super Cool: The stitches on a baseball are sewn by hand!

Superstar Quiz

Before we jump in, let's find out where you are on the path to baseball greatness. Answer these questions honestly (no peeking at your friend's answers!):

1. Do you spend more time playing MLB The Show than actually playing baseball?
2. Have you ever tried to catch a pop fly and ended up wearing it as a hat?
3. Does your dog field ground balls better than you do?
4. Do you sleep with your glove under your pillow hoping the skills will sink in overnight?

If you answered "yes" to any of these, don't worry! You're in exactly the right place. Even the biggest stars had to start somewhere.

More Fun Facts!

- Amazing!: Some MLB players can read the label on a spinning baseball!
- Wild Stuff: The first baseball game used a fence post as a bat!
- Cool Beans: Baseball gloves can last for over 20 years!

Your Baseball Identity

Every great player needs their own style. You don't have to copy anyone else -

you can be your own kind of awesome! Think about it:

- Are you "The Vacuum" (sucks up every ground ball in sight)?
- Maybe "The Spider" (catches everything in your web)?
- Or "The Rocket" (throws heat but sometimes to the wrong zip code)?

Pick your style and own it! Just maybe don't call yourself "The GOAT" yet - let's work up to that one.

How "The Splendid Splinter" Got His Name!

Ted Williams wasn't just skinny - he was PENCIL thin! When he first showed up to play for the Boston Red Sox, reporters couldn't believe such a beanpole of a kid could hit with such EXPLOSIVE power! At 6'3" but only 170 pounds soaking wet, Williams looked like he might snap in half during a strong wind! But when he swung that bat - KA-BOOM! The ball would rocket off his bat like it was shot from a cannon! One sportswriter watching his thin frame unleash such mighty hits called him "The Splendid Splinter" in a newspaper article, and the perfect nickname stuck faster than bubble gum on a dugout bench! Williams didn't mind the teasing about his skinny build because his bat did all the talking - splinter or not, he became one of the greatest hitters baseball has eve

First Steps to Greatness

Here's your first mission (should you choose to accept it):

1. Find a baseball (a rolled-up sock works too, but don't tell anyone I

said that)

2. Find some space (your backyard works, but maybe warn Mom about her flowers first)

3. Start practicing basic skills (this means throwing and catching without closing your eyes)\

Emergency Situations!

When You Throw the Ball Over the Fence:

- Stay calm
- Have a backup ball ready
- Blame it on the wind
- Be nice to your neighbor (you'll probably need their help a lot

NEXT LEVEL SKILLS

The Two-Glove Master

- Practice catching with both hands
- Switch hit during tee practice
- Field grounders with either hand

The Sock Ball Specialist

- Create different size sock balls
- Practice in your room
- Perfect your form without breaking windows (see below)

Perfecting Your Form: Your Baseball Building Blocks!

Your baseball form is like your secret superhero stance - get it right and AMAZING things happen!

Whether you're pitching, hitting, or fielding, your feet are your foundation! Place them just right - not too close, not too wide. Like a tree with strong roots, good foot position gives you POWER and BALANCE!

Watch how your favorite MLB stars move in slow motion. Notice how their bodies flow like water? Each part moves in perfect order - hips THEN shoulders THEN arms. It's like a chain reaction of awesome!

Practice in front of a mirror or have a friend take video. What you THINK you look like and what you ACTUALLY look like might be totally different! This is how the pros get better - they study themselves!

Remember, perfect form feels weird at first - that's normal! Your muscles need time to learn these new moves. Keep practicing, and soon your perfect baseball form will feel as natural as breathing. That's when the magic really happens!

The Focus Master

- Practice with distractions
- Field balls while someone calls out math problems
- Throw to targets while music plays

Cool Story: The Midnight Pitcher

Shohei Ohtani had a SECRET that nobody knew about. While other kids were sleeping, 12-year-old Shohei would sneak out to his backyard in Japan at MIDNIGHT with a flashlight, a ball, and his glove.

In the darkness, with just a tiny circle of light on a homemade target, Shohei would practice pitching for HOURS! But he didn't stop there - after pitching, he'd grab his bat and hit balls off a tee in the dark! The neighbors thought their yard was haunted because all they heard were mysterious "THWACK!" sounds in the middle of the night!

At school, teachers couldn't figure out why Shohei was always sleepy. His baseball coach was confused too - how was this kid getting so AMAZING at both pitching AND hitting?

The truth stayed Shohei's secret until his team made it to the championship. When the game went into extra innings and the lights failed at the field, everyone panicked. Everyone except Shohei.

"I can play in the dark," he said calmly.

While other players squinted and struggled, Shohei pitched a perfect inning, then hit the game-winning home run as if the darkness was his special super-power!

Years later, when Shohei Ohtani became the first modern baseball superstar who could both pitch AND hit at an elite level, surprising the entire Major Leagues, reporters would ask how he did it. He'd just smile and say, "I had some extra practice time that nobody knew about."

Pro Secret! Some MLB players practice throwing and catching with tennis balls to improve their reactions!

Warning! Start with the basics before trying any fancy stuff. Even pros still practice the simple things!

P.S. If your parents ask why you're throwing sock balls in your room, tell them you're "developing hand-eye coordination through textile-based spherical manipulation." Then run away before they ask what that means!

Remember: Every great player started somewhere. Today, that somewhere is right here, with you, reading this book. Now get out there and show the world what you've got!

Chapter 2

The Throw Down (Forget Throwing Like Anyone Else)

Alright, future flamethrower, it's time to learn how to make that baseball go where you want it to (instead of toward Mrs. Johnson's prized petunias). Maybe right now your throws look more like a wild sprinkler system than a laser beam. Maybe you've developed a reputation as the kid who keeps all the neighbors on their toes - literally.

That old saying "you throw like a girl" needs to go away anyway - have you seen softball pitchers? They're amazing! What matters is learning to throw like YOU, but better. Whether you're throwing like a wet noodle or just need some fine-tuning, we're about to turn you into a throwing machine!

The best part? Every great player started by throwing balls all over the place. Even the pros had to learn the difference between "throw it home" and "throw it into the next county." Time to turn those wild throws into perfect strikes!

Fun Facts That'll Blow Your Mind!

- Did you know? The fastest recorded throw was 105.8 mph!
- Wow Factor: A baseball spins over 1,500 times during one pitch!
- Mind Blown: MLB pitchers release the ball in less than half a second!
- Super Cool: Some throws from the outfield travel over 300 feet!

The Basic Throw-Down

The Perfect Grip:

- Find the seams (they're the red stitchy parts)

- Hold it like an egg (not a squished grape)
- Keep your fingers relaxed (no death grips!)

The Power Position:

- Stand sideways (like you're stuck between two walls)
- Point your glove at your target (not at the sky)
- Step and throw (don't fall over!

More Fun Facts!

- Amazing!: Outfielders' throws can stay in the air for over 3 seconds!
- Wild Stuff: Some catchers can throw to second base in 1.9 seconds!
- Cool Beans: Players throw about 100-200 times per game!

Emergency Situations!

When Your Throw Goes Wild:

- Yell "HEADS UP!" (really loud!)
- Act like you meant to do that
- Have a backup ball ready
- Practice your "sorry" wave

When You Can't Find the Strike Zone:

- Take a deep breath
- Aim for your target's chest
- Pretend you're playing darts
- Remember: Even pros throw balls sometimes

The Accuracy Game

Try these challenges:

1. Set up targets (not your little brother)
2. Start close, move back slowly
3. Make it a competition with friends
4. Keep score (be honest!)

Pro Tips That Actually Work:

1. Follow through toward your target
2. Keep your elbow above your shoulder
3. Practice every day (yes, every single day!)
4. Start slow, speed comes later

NEXT LEVEL SKILLS

The Quick-Draw

- Practice catching and throwing in one motion
- Work on different arm angles
- Develop your sidearm throw for special plays

The Accuracy Master

- Set up multiple targets
- Practice throwing to different spots
- Work on changing speeds

The Position Pro

- Learn throws from different positions
- Practice throwing while moving
- Master the crow hop (below)

The Crow Hop

The crow hop is a special move that outfielders use when they need to throw the ball really far.

Imagine you catch a ball in the outfield and need to throw it all the way to home plate. Instead of just standing still and throwing, you take a little hop forward first - that's the crow hop! This hop helps you put more power into your throw, kind of like how you might take a few steps before jumping to jump farther.

When you crow hop, you:

- Take a small jump forward after catching the ball
- Move your weight from your back foot to your front foot
- Turn your body as you throw
- This all helps you throw the ball harder and more accurately!

Outfielders use this move all the time to make those long throws when trying to get runners out.

Pro Secret! Some MLB infielders practice their throws with their eyes closed to perfect their mechanics!

Warning! Never try sidearm or submarine throws until you've mastered the basic overhand throw!

A submarine throw is a special way of pitching where you throw the ball from down low, almost like you're sweeping the ground.

Instead of throwing overhand like most pitchers, a submarine pitcher bends way down and throws the ball upward from below their knees. Their arm swings up like it's coming from underwater - that's why it's called "submarine"!

When you throw submarine style:

- You bend your knees a lot
- Your throwing arm swings up from very low
- The ball travels upward toward the batter
- This makes the ball move differently and can be really tricky to hit!

Submarine pitchers look funny when they throw, but this unusual style can confuse batters because they're not used to seeing the ball come from that angle.

Final Fun Facts!

- Cool!: Some outfielders can throw a ball from the warning track to home plate in the air!
- Wow!: Catchers practice throwing 100+ times per day!
- Amazing!: The longest recorded throw was 445 feet and 10 inches!

P.S. If anyone asks why you're throwing at targets all day, tell them you're "calculating trajectory variables for optimal spherical projectile placement." Then show off your awesome new throwing skills while they're trying to figure out what you just said!

Remember: Great throws aren't born, they're made - one practice session at a time! Keep at it, future star!

Chapter 3

Hitting Heroes (How to Hit the Ball Instead of the Air!)

Stand in the batter's box. Take a deep breath. Try not to think about everyone watching. Ignore the fact that your batting helmet is slightly too big and keeps falling over your eyes. This is your moment! Well, it would be your moment if you could just make contact with the ball instead of creating a cool breeze with your bat.

Don't worry - every great hitter started by missing more balls than they hit. Even Babe Ruth struck out 1,330 times! (Though he probably didn't have to deal with a wobbly helmet.) The difference between good hitters and great ones isn't just talent - it's understanding how to turn those mighty whiffs into solid hits.

Right now, you might be swinging like you're trying to swat flies with a pool noodle, but that's about to change. Whether you're dreaming of hitting towering home runs or just want to stop striking out in front of your crush (we've all been there), this chapter is your ticket to hitting greatness!

Fun Facts That'll Blow Your Mind!

- Did you know? The longest home run ever measured traveled 582 feet!
- Wow Factor: A baseball comes off the bat faster than a car on the highway!
- Mind Blown: The best hitters can see the baseball's seams spinning!
- Super Cool: Some MLB bats cost more than 300 video game

Hall of Fame Home Run Story: Babe Ruth's Called Shot

Picture this: It's the 1932 World Series. Babe Ruth steps up to bat. The crowd is going wild, but not in a good way - they're actually making fun of him! So what does the Babe do? He points to the outfield bleachers, like he's saying "I'm going to hit it right there!" And then... BOOM! He actually does it! A home run exactly where he pointed!

The crazy part? He was eating hot dogs before the game. (Maybe not the best pre-game meal, but hey, it worked for him!

The Hitting Basics

The Perfect Stance:

- Stand like a superhero (balanced and ready)
- Hold the bat like you're shaking hands (not strangling it)
- Keep your eyes forward (the ball's not in the dugout!)

The Sweet Swing:

- Start with your hands back
- Step towards the pitcher
- Swing level (we're not chopping wood!)
- Follow through (pose for the cameras!

Emergency Situations!

When You Keep Striking Out:

- Remember: Even the best hitters fail 7 out of 10 times
- Take a deep breath
- Focus on the ball (not your embarrassed mom)
- Pretend the last pitch never happened

When You Hit It Off the Tee... Backward:

- Act like you were just warming up
- Adjust your stance
- Try again (maybe with less power this time)
- Remember: Tees never laugh at you

NEXT LEVEL SKILLS

The Contact King

- Practice hitting to all fields
- Work on two-strike approaches
- Master the art of fouling off tough pitches (see below)

Master the Art of Fouling Off Tough Pitches: Your Baseball Survival Skill!

When the pitcher throws that PERFECT pitch on a two-strike count, it's time to unleash your secret weapon - the BATTLE FOUL TIP! Top hitters aren't just good at crushing mistakes, they're EXPERTS at staying alive when the pitcher makes a great pitch!

With two strikes, choke up on the bat like you're gripping a magic wand and shorten your swing. Don't try to crush it - just TOUCH it! A tiny tap that sends the ball screaming into the seats counts the same as a 400-foot foul ball! Each foul ball is like telling the pitcher, "Nice try, but I'm NOT going down that easy!"

Watch how the pros do it - they'll fight off five, six, SEVEN tough pitches in a row! Each foul makes the pitcher work harder and might force a mistake on the next throw. It's like a staring contest - and you're NOT blinking first! The greatest batting superpower isn't just hitting home runs - it's SURVIVING tough pitches until you get one you can handle!

The Power Pro

- Develop your home run swing
- Learn to drive the ball (see below)
- Practice hitting for distance

Learning to Drive the Ball: Unlock Your Batting POWER!

Forget those wimpy little bloops - it's time to learn how to DRIVE the ball like the big leaguers! Hitting for power isn't about swinging harder - it's about swinging SMARTER!

The secret starts in your legs - they're your baseball power generators! Push hard against the ground like you're trying to crack it open. That force travels up through your hips (the REAL home run muscle!), into your shoulders, and finally EXPLODES through the bat!

Don't just swing AT the ball - swing THROUGH it! Imagine the baseball is actually sitting 6 inches PAST where you see it. When you follow through like this, the ball jumps off your bat like it was shot from a cannon!

Remember, timing beats strength EVERY time! A perfectly timed swing from a smaller player will drive the ball farther than a muscle-bound giant with bad timing. Watch the ball ALL the way from the pitcher's hand, and when everything clicks - BOOM! That beautiful sound of a perfectly driven ball will have everyone's heads turning to watch your hit sail through the air!

The Situational Star

- Learn to bunt (yes, it's actually important)
- Practice hit-and-run swings
- Master the sacrifice fly (see below)

The Sacrifice Fly: Be a Team Hero Without a Hit!

A sacrifice fly might not show up as a hit in YOUR stats, but it's worth its weight in GOLD to your team! This special play is like being a secret agent - you're giving yourself up for the greater good!

When there's a runner on third base with less than two outs, your mission changes. Forget trying to get a hit - just get that ball DEEP into the outfield! Swing slightly upward to create a high fly ball that travels far enough to let your teammate tag up and race home!

The best part? Even though you're out, you DON'T get charged with an at-bat in your batting average! It's like a free chance to help your team score! And when your teammate crosses home plate because of YOUR sacrifice fly, that RBI goes on YOUR stats!

Remember, baseball isn't just about personal glory - it's about doing whatever helps the TEAM win! When coach gives you the "sac fly" sign, stand tall and proud knowing you're about to become the unsung hero your team needs! Who needs a base hit when you can deliver a run with one mighty swing to the sky?

Cool Story: The Backwards Batter

Everyone laughed when Rickey Henderson stepped into the batter's box for the first time in Little League. Instead of standing the normal way, little Rickey stood with his back almost FACING the pitcher! His feet were practically pointing at the shortstop!

"HEY KID! You're doing it all wrong!" parents shouted from the bleachers.

Even his coach ran out, trying to turn Rickey around properly. "You can't hit like that!" he insisted.

But Rickey just smiled and said, "Watch me."

The first pitch came in FAST. Rickey's weird stance looked so awkward that the pitcher thought this would be an easy strikeout. But when the ball crossed the plate, Rickey's bat WHIPPED around with lightning speed! CRACK! The ball shot between two outfielders and rolled all the way to the fence!

As Rickey stood on second base with a double, his coach scratched his head in amazement. "How did you even SEE the ball from that strange position?"

"That's my secret," Rickey explained. "When I was really little, I practiced swinging at bottle caps that my brothers would throw at me. They'd throw from all different angles, so I learned to hit from ANY position!"

Rickey kept his strange, crouched, backwards-looking stance all the way to the Major Leagues, where he became one of baseball's greatest leadoff hitters ever! Pitchers would stare in confusion at his weird stance, thinking it would be impossible to hit that way. But just when they thought they had an easy out, WHAM! Rickey's bat would flash through the zone, sending the ball flying as he raced toward first base!

Sometimes the strangest-looking techniques work the best – Rickey Henderson proved that being different can make you a superstar!

Pro Secret! Some MLB players practice hitting with a Wiffle ball to perfect their swing path!

Warning! Power is great, but contact comes first. Don't try to hit home runs until you can consistently make contact!

More Fun Facts!

- Amazing!: The fastest pitch ever hit was 123.9 mph off the bat!
- Wild Stuff: Some players can hit a baseball thrown at 100 mph!
- Cool Beans: MLB players break about 120 bats per season!

P.S. If your coach asks why you're practicing your home run trot before learning to hit, tell them you're "preparing for future success through positive visualization techniques." Then go practice your actual swing!

Remember: Every great hitter started by missing the ball completely. Keep swinging, slugger!

Chapter 4

The Glove Guru (Because Ground Balls Shouldn't Be Scary)

Slide your hand into that baseball glove. Feel how stiff it is? It's like trying to catch with a pizza box! Your coach keeps yelling "Two hands!" but you're too busy fighting with your glove like it's your little brother stealing the TV remote.

Don't panic - every Gold Glove winner started with a glove that felt like a foreign object! Even Ozzie Smith (nicknamed "The Wizard" for his amazing defense) dropped plenty of balls when he was a kid. The difference between good fielders and AMAZING ones isn't just quick hands - it's becoming best friends with your glove!

Right now, you might be stabbing at grounders like you're trying to catch butterflies with a waffle iron, but that's about to change! Whether you're dreaming of making diving catches or just want to stop balls from rolling between your legs (while EVERYONE is watching), this chapter is your secret path to fielding fame!

Fun Facts That'll Blow Your Mind!

- Did you know? Baseball gloves used to be about the size of your hand!
- Wow Factor: Some MLB players use the same glove for over 5 years!
- Mind Blown: Infielders catch balls going over 100 mph!
- Super Cool: Outfielders' gloves are like catching pizzas while infielders' are like catching tacos!

The Fielding Fundamentals

Ground Ball Guru:

- Get in front of the ball (it's not going to bite!)
- Create a triangle with your feet and glove
- Watch it into your glove (no peeking!)
- Field through the ball (like scooping ice cream)

Pop Fly Pro:

- Call for the ball (louder than your mom calls for dinner)
- Get under it early (don't do the panic dance)
- Two hands! (one hand catches are for showing off)
- Squeeze it like your favorite stuffed animal

Emergency Situations!

When The Ball Takes a Crazy Hop:

- Block it with your body
- Keep the ball in front
- Pretend you meant to catch it that way

- Dive!

When You Lose It In The Sun:

- Don't panic (okay, maybe panic a little)
- Use your glove for shade
- Pray to the baseball gods
- Have a good excuse ready

NEXT LEVEL SKILLS

The Backhand Bandit

- Practice fielding from all angles
- Master the backhand scoop (see below)
- Learn to throw from different positions

The Backhand Scoop: Your Secret Fielding Superpower!

When that grounder zips toward your glove side, don't panic - it's time for your BACKHAND SCOOP!

Shift your body quick like a ninja and get that glove down LOW. Your glove should sweep the ground like you're scooping ice cream from the bottom of the container!

Keep your palm facing UP and fingers pointed DOWN at the dirt. This creates your magic "scoop zone" where grounders can't escape!

The secret weapon? Your other hand! Bring it close to block any sneaky bounces, ready to trap the ball if needed. Two hands are better than one!

Remember, even if you miss sometimes, great infielders keep trying their backhand scoop. Practice makes perfect, and soon you'll be snagging grounders like they're moving in slow motion

The Diving Dynamo

- Start with sliding catches
- Progress to controlled dives
- Perfect the pop-up throw (see below)

The Perfect Pop-Up Throw: Your Rocket Launch Sequence!

When that sky-high pop-up heads your way, get ready for your special catching-and-throwing combo move!

Position yourself UNDER the ball with your feet shoulder-width apart, like a superhero about to take off! As the ball drops from the clouds, catch it with two hands right in front of your throwing shoulder - that's your launch pad!

The MAGIC happens next! As soon as the ball hits your glove, your feet should already be moving. Your body turns like a spring uncoiling, and your throwing hand grabs the ball in one smooth motion!

No time for fancy moves here - your throw should blast off FAST! Think:

Catch, Turn, Fire! Like a human rocket launcher sending the ball exactly where it needs to go!

The best fielders make it look easy, but they've practiced this a thousand times. Master your pop-up throw, and you'll amaze everyone with how quickly you can catch and fire that ball to the right base.

The Wall Walker

- Practice tracking balls near fences
- Learn to gauge your distance
- Master the warning track (see below)

Mastering the Warning Track: Your Outfield Safety Zone!

Racing back for that deep fly ball? Listen for the CRUNCH under your feet! That special sound means you've hit the warning track - your secret signal that the wall is coming!

When you feel that different surface, quick-peek over your shoulder but DON'T slow down! Like a spy on a mission, you need to know where the wall is while still tracking the ball against the sky.

The warning track is your friend, not something scary! Count your steps when you feel that crunch - "One, two, THREE!" Now you know exactly how many steps until CRASH! Soon you'll have your own warning track radar!

The bravest outfielders know when to go full speed and when to put on the brakes. Practice makes perfect, so chase those practice flies all the way to the track. Remember, catching the ball is awesome, but coming home without bruises is even bette

Pro Secret! Some outfielders practice catching with their eyes closed to get a better feel for their glove!

Warning! No fancy plays until you've mastered the basics. Web gems are cool, but routine plays win games!

More Fun Facts!

- Amazing!: Some gloves cost more than 300 cheeseburgers!
- Wild Stuff: MLB players oil their gloves like they're giving them a spa day!
- Cool Beans: The biggest MLB glove allowed is 13 inches!

Quick Tips:

1. Break in your glove properly (not under your mattress)
2. Keep your glove clean (that's not what dirt is for)
3. Always be ready (even when you're daydreaming about nachos)
4. Practice barehanded when safe

P.S. If anyone asks why you're rolling around in the grass catching pop flies, tell them you're "studying gravitational physics through leather-assisted spherical object interception." Then make an awesome catch while they're scratching their heads!

Remember: Every great fielder started by taking one off the nose. Keep your glove down and your chin up!

Chapter 5

Baseball Brilliance (Your Brain: The Most Important Muscle in Baseball)

Think baseball's all about muscle? Think again! While you're out there flexing in front of the mirror practicing your home run trot (we see you!), it's time to start flexing the most important muscle in baseball - your brain!

Maybe you're the kind of player who forgets how many outs there are, or sometimes runs to third base instead of first (hey, they both look the same from home plate!). Or maybe you're already a student of the game but want to understand why your coach keeps yelling about "situations" and "baseball IQ."

It's time to turn your baseball brain from a flip phone into a smartphone! Even if you think strategy is just something they talk about in boring baseball movies, you're about to discover how being baseball-smart can make you look like a genius on the field (even if you still can't remember your multiplication tables).

Fun Facts That'll Blow Your Mind!

- Did you know? MLB managers make about 150 decisions per game!
- Wow Factor: Batters have less than 0.4 seconds to decide to swing!
- Mind Blown: Fielders process 20+ factors before each pitch!
- Super Cool: Catchers know over 100 different pitch combinations!

The Baseball Brain Basics

Field Vision:

- Watch the batter's stance
- Notice where fielders are playing
- Spot the gaps (that's where hits live!)
- Think ahead (like a baseball time traveler

Game Smarts:

- Count the outs (seriously, always know the outs)
- Know the score (not just when you're winning)
- Understand situations (when to be a hero, when to play it safe)
- Read the defense (they're trying to trick you!)

Emergency Situations!

When You Forget How Many Outs:

- Look at the scoreboard (sneakily)
- Check what other fielders are doing
- Ask your teammate (whisper it!)

- Learn from it (but pretend you knew all along)

When You Can't Remember The Signs:

- Stay cool (don't do the confused puppy look)
- Ask for them again
- Have a backup plan
- Remember: Even pros mess these up!

NEXT LEVEL SKILLS

The Strategy Master

- Learn to read defensive positions
- Predict where the ball will be hit
- Understand pitch sequences (see below)

Pitch Sequences: Baseball's Secret Code!

Pitchers aren't just throwing the ball - they're telling a story! Each pitch is like a piece of a puzzle.

First comes the FASTBALL - ZOOM! Right down the middle. The batter thinks, "I'll hit the next one!"

But wait! Here comes the CURVEBALL - WHOOSH! It starts high then

DIVES like a roller coaster!

Then the sneaky CHANGEUP - it looks fast but arrives S-L-O-W-L-Y, making batters swing too early. "Gotcha!"

The best pitchers mix these up like a magician's trick. Maybe fastball, fastball, then SURPRISE - slider that darts away like a scared rabbit!

Remember, it's not just about throwing hard - it's about keeping the batter guessing. That's the secret code of pitching!

The Baseball Computer

- Memorize common game situations
- Learn what each position does on every play
- Master the mental side of base running (see below)

The Mental Side of Base Running

Running the bases isn't just about being fast - it's about being SMART!

When you're on base, be like a detective watching for clues. How quick is the pitcher's move to first? Is the catcher's throw strong? These are your secret weapons!

Count the seconds between pitches and PLAN your steal. Trust your instincts - when that little voice says "GO!" that's your moment!

Remember, even the fastest runners get caught sometimes. The best base stealers aren't worried about making mistakes - they learn and get better each time!

Base running is a game of chess - think two steps ahead, and you'll be sliding into home before they know what happened!

The Field General

- Know where to throw before the ball is hit
- Learn cut-off positions for every situation
- Master defensive alignments (see below)

Mastering Defensive Alignment

Playing defense isn't just standing in one spot - it's like being a superhero who knows where the ball will go before it's hit!

Watch how the batter stands. Do they swing late? Move toward right field! Do they hit grounders? Step in closer! Each batter gives away secret clues about where they'll hit.

Talk to your teammates like you're all connected by invisible string. "I've got it!" "Back me up!" "Shift left!" These magic words keep everyone working together.

Remember the situation - how many outs? Runner on first? Your position might need to change! Like a chess player, think about what could happen NEXT.

The best defenders aren't always the fastest - they're the smartest! They position themselves in the perfect spot and make hard plays look EASY!

Pro Secret! Some MLB players play chess between games to improve their strategic thinking!

Warning! Don't overthink it! Baseball brain power is great, but don't forget to actually play the game!

More Fun Facts!

- Amazing!: Catchers use over 25 different hand signals!
- Wild Stuff: Teams steal signs from 200+ feet away!
- Cool Beans: Some plays involve all 9 players at once!

Quick Tips:

1. Always think "What if?" before each pitch
2. Know your job on every type of play
3. Watch what other players do
4. Learn from your mistakes (there will be plenty!)

P.S. If your coach asks why you're standing still staring at the field, tell them you're "analyzing multi-variable defensive alignment optimization scenarios." Then make a smart baseball play while they're trying to figure out what that means!

Remember: Baseball isn't just played with your body - it's played with your brain! Keep thinking, future strategist!

Chapter 6

Dugout Domination (How to Be the Teammate Everyone High-Fives)

Welcome to your home away from home - the dugout! This is where memories are made, rallies are started, and about 47 pounds of sunflower seeds are systematically destroyed per game. Whether you're a dugout DJ leading the rally chants or the quiet kid who organizes the batting helmets, it's time to learn the art of being an awesome teammate.

Right now, you might be the player who sits alone wondering if anyone noticed your three strikeouts, or maybe you're the one trying to start the wave with two outs in the last inning. Either way, the dugout is more than just a place to sit between innings - it's where championship teams are built!

Being a great teammate isn't just about high-fives and "good game" comments (though those are pretty important). It's about learning how to support your fellow players, keep the energy up when things are down, and yes, even help clean up those sunflower seed shells after the game. Time to become the teammate everyone wants to sit next to!Fun Facts That'll Blow Your Mind!

- Did you know? MLB teams go through 1,000+ pounds of sunflower seeds per season!
- Wow Factor: Dugouts can hold over 40 people and 100 bubble gum pieces!
- Mind Blown: Some teams have secret handshakes for every player!
- Super Cool: Players chew through 300+ pieces of gum per game!

Team Player Tale: Lou Gehrig's Iron Horse Story

Ever heard of Lou Gehrig? This guy played in 2,130 straight games! That's like playing every single day for 14 years - no sick days, no vacation, not even a "my dog ate my baseball cleats" day. Once, he got hit in the head by a pitch and just shook it off like it was a raindrop. The next day? He hit two home runs!

But here's the cool part - he never complained, always supported his teammates, and played his hardest every single day. That's why they called him the Iron Horse. (Though if you ask us, Iron Horse sounds more like a superhero than a baseball player - which, come to think of it, he kind of was!)

The Dugout Code

The Perfect Teammate:

- Cheer for others (louder than your mom at your games)
- Help with equipment (even if it's not yours)
- Pay attention (no playing phone games!)
- Be ready when needed (yes, even if you're the backup to the backup)

Emergency Situations!

When Your Team Is Losing:

- Keep the energy up
- Start a rally chant

- No blame game (even if Bobby missed that easy fly ball)
- Be the positive one

When You're Not Playing:

- Stay in the game mentally
- Chart pitches (look smart!)
- Be ready to go in
- Support your teammates (like a human cheerleader)

NEXT LEVEL SKILLS

The Energy Expert

- Create team rally calls
- Design unique celebrations
- Master the art of dugout organization (see below)

Dugout Organization: The Secret Clubhouse!

Your dugout is like a superhero headquarters - keeping it organized helps your team win!

Every bat, helmet, and glove needs a special spot. Line up your bats by size like soldiers ready for battle! Hang helmets where you can grab them in a flash!

Know the batting order ahead of time. Who's up next? Who's "on deck"? Be ready when it's your turn - no scrambling for equipment!

Coaches love players who help keep water bottles filled and equipment tidy. Be that teammate! It shows you care about more than just your own game.

The neatest dugouts belong to the winning teams! A clean, organized dugout means clear minds ready to play their best. Remember: championship teams have championship dugouts

The Team Builder

- Learn everyone's signals
- Help new players feel welcome
- Become the go-to encouragement guy/gal

The Dugout Director

- Keep track of the lineup
- Help coaches with equipment
- Master the art of staying ready (see below)

Staying Ready in the Dugout: The Hidden Game!

The dugout isn't just a waiting room - it's where secret baseball powers are charged up!

Watch every pitch like a hawk studying its prey. Notice how the pitcher throws to lefties vs. righties. Is the catcher showing signs? These clues will help when it's YOUR turn!

Keep your body moving between innings - quick stretches, light jumps, or arm swings. Like a tiger ready to pounce, your muscles should stay warm!

Play "What Would I Do?" for each situation. "If the ball comes to me here, I'll throw THERE." Your brain needs practice just like your swing does!

The best players aren't just playing when they're on the field - they're ALWAYS in the game, even from the dugout. Stay focused, stay ready, and you'll shine when your moment comes!

Pro Secret! Some MLB teams have a different secret handshake for every possible situation in a game!

Warning! Don't be the dugout clown when it's time to be serious. Know when to joke and when to focus!

More Fun Facts!

- Amazing!: Some dugouts have secret candy stashes!
- Wild Stuff: Teams can go through 40 pounds of bubble gum per month!
- Cool Beans: Players create new celebrations before every season!

P.S. If anyone asks why you're organizing the dugout like a military base, tell them you're "implementing advanced team chemistry enhancement protocols through systematic environmental optimization." Then give them a high-five while they try to understand what you just said!

Remember: Great teammates become legends, even if they're not the star players. Keep the energy up, future team captain!

Chapter 7

Game Day Greatness (Turn Those Butterflies Into Base Hits)

This is it - game day! The sun's shining (or maybe it's raining, who knows), the grass is green, and your stomach feels like it's doing more flips than an Olympic gymnast. Your uniform is crisp (until you dive for that first ball), your cleats are tied (double-knotted because you learned that lesson), and you've only put your socks on backwards twice this morning.

But here's the thing about game day - it's exactly what you've been practicing for! All those backyard catches, the batting practice where you hit more air than ball, and those grounders that sometimes hit you in funny places? They're about to pay off.

You might be thinking: "But what if I mess up? What if I strike out? What if I throw the ball over the first baseman's head and it lands in someone's hot dog?" First off, that hot dog probably needed more excitement anyway. Second, every single MLB player - yes, even the ones with million-dollar contracts - has been exactly where you are right now.

Think about it: Before they were stars, they were just kids with butterflies in their stomachs, dreams in their heads, and occasionally backwards socks on their feet. The difference? They learned how to turn those pre-game jitters into game-time awesome. And that's exactly what you're about to learn!

Fun Facts That'll Blow Your Mind!

- Did you know? Some MLB players eat the exact same meal before every game!
- Wow Factor: Players have up to 12 different pre-game rituals!
- Mind Blown: Some batters adjust their batting gloves 6 times before EVERY pitch!

- Super Cool: Teams use over 60 baseballs in one game!

Pre-Game Power

The Night Before:

- Get good sleep (no staying up playing MLB The Show!)
- Pack your bag (check for both cleats this time)
- Lay out your uniform (wearing it to bed doesn't give you extra powers)

Game Day Menu:

- Eat smart (no five-alarm tacos before the game)
- Stay hydrated (but not so much you need a bathroom break every inning)
- Arrive early (it's the only time your parents won't mind rushing)

Emergency Situations!

When You're Super Nervous:

- Take deep breaths
- Remember: It's just a game (a really fun one!)

- Focus on one play at a time
- Pretend you're practicing in the backyard

When Things Go Wrong:

- Stay positive (no throwing gloves!)
- Remember: Next play is your play
- Keep your head up (the ground isn't that interesting)
- Trust your practice

NEXT LEVEL SKILLS

The Routine Master

- Develop your own pre-game ritual
- Create a batting box routine
- Perfect your between-innings warmup (see below)

Between-Inning Warm-Up: The Secret Recharge!

Those few minutes between innings aren't just a break - they're your superhero power-up time!

Infielders, snap those throws around the horn like lightning bolts! Each perfect throw tells your teammates, "I'm READY for anything!" Your glove hand should feel hot and your arm loose.

Outfielders, use those warm-up tosses to check the wind and sun. Is the breeze pushing balls toward right field? Now you know your secret advantage!

Pitchers, those eight warm-up pitches are golden! Start with easy throws, then build up. Feel the mound, check your grip, and find your target. Like a race car driver testing the track!

Remember, great teams look SHARP during warm-ups. When the other team sees your quick, clean throws, they'll know they're in for a tough game. Your between-inning routine shows everyone you mean business!

The Focus Finder

- Practice blocking out distractions
- Learn to reset between pitches (see below)
- Master the art of staying calm

Resetting Between Pitches

The space between pitches isn't empty time - it's your magical reset button!

When you're batting, step out of the box and take a deep breath. Wipe away the last pitch like erasing a chalkboard. Bad swing? POOF! It's gone! Good players have short memories!

Pitchers, walk around the mound after each throw. Touch your cap, adjust your glove - these little moves are your brain's way of saying "Next pitch is a fresh start!"

Talk to yourself with power words: "Ready!" "Focus!" "See it!" These magic spells help chase away nervous thoughts and keep your superhero baseball powers strong!

Remember, baseball isn't just played with muscles - it's played between your ears! The champions aren't the ones who never make mistakes - they're the ones who know how to reset and try again with a clear mind

The Game Face Pro

- Handle pressure situations
- Maintain energy all game
- Lead by example

Cool Story: The Invisible Catcher's Signal

Nobody could figure out how little José Altuve always seemed to know what pitch was coming. At just 4'6" in seventh grade, he was the smallest player in the league, but somehow he was hitting EVERYTHING!

Fastballs, curveballs, sliders – it didn't matter. His tiny bat would find the ball and send it screaming into the outfield! Coaches started whispering that something fishy was going on.

"He's got someone signaling from the stands!" one accused. "He's peeking at the catcher's signs!" said another.

The truth came out during the championship game. With two strikes, the opposing pitcher threw his nastiest curveball – the one that had fooled EVERYONE all season. But José crushed it over the left field fence!

After the game, José's teammate finally spilled the beans. "It's his EARS!" he explained. "José can actually HEAR the ball!"

José had spent hours practicing with his eyes closed, just listening to different pitches cutting through the air. A fastball made a different sound than a curveball. A slider whistled while a changeup whooshed! By the time the ball was halfway to the plate, José's incredible ears had already told him exactly what was coming!

Years later, when José Altuve became one of baseball's most feared hitters despite being the shortest player in the Major Leagues, pitchers never knew he was listening to their pitches sing through the air!

Pro Secret! Some MLB players visualize success while listening to their favorite song before every game!

Warning! Don't let your routine become more important than your performance!

More Fun Facts!

- Amazing!: Players can lose 8 pounds in water weight during a game!
- Wild Stuff: Some pitchers won't step on the foul line... ever!
- Cool Beans: Teams have secret signals just for emergencies!

Quick Tips:

1. Have a routine (but don't go crazy)
2. Stay in the game mentally
3. Support your teammates
4. Have fun (yes, that's actually important!)

P.S. If anyone asks why you're doing your special pre-game dance, tell them you're "activating optimal neuromuscular pathways through rhythmic preparatory movements." Then go get a hit while they're trying to decode what you just said!

Remember: Game day isn't about being perfect - it's about playing hard and having fun! Let's play ball!

Chapter 8

Speed, Slides & Steals (Because Running in Circles Can Be Strategic!)

Alright, future base-stealing sensation! Time to learn how to turn those base paths into your personal race track. Maybe right now you run the bases like you're on a casual stroll through the park, or maybe you're so fast you sometimes forget to actually touch the bases (speed is nothing without the stops!).

You've probably seen those MLB highlights where players seem to float around the bases, sliding into second like ninjas and taking extra bases like they're stealing candy from a baby (which you shouldn't do, by the way). But here's a secret - even Rickey Henderson had to learn which base was which before he could steal 1,406 of them!

Whether you're trying to stop running with your eyes closed or ready to learn how to slide without eating a pound of dirt, this chapter is your guide to becoming a base path boss. Time to turn those "should I go?" moments into "try to stop me" opportunities!

Fun Facts That'll Blow Your Mind!

- Did you know? The fastest MLB player can run from home to first in 3.7 seconds!
- Wow Factor: Base stealers study pitchers' moves for hours!
- Mind Blown: Players can reach speeds of over 20 mph on the bases!
- Super Cool: Some players steal home plate at 30 feet per second!

Base Running Basics

The Perfect Lead:

- Take enough steps (but not so many your coach has a heart attack)
- Stay balanced (no flamingo poses)
- Watch the pitcher (he's probably watching you)
- Be ready to move (like a cat waiting to pounce)

The Slide Master:

- Start your slide late (better than never)
- Keep your head up (the base is hard)
- Tuck those arms (unless you like grass stains)
- Pop up ready to run (looking cool is a bonus)

Emergency Situations!

When You Get Caught in a Rundown (a rundown is like a game of tag between bases, where fielders try to chase and tag a runner who got caught between two bases before they can safely reach either one):

- Don't panic (much)
- Change directions (a lot)

- Make the fielders throw (they might get tired)
- Hope for a miracle (it happens!)

When You Slide Past the Base:

- Grab the base (quick!)
- Act casual (like you meant to do that)
- Get up smoothly (or at least try)
- Learn from it

NEXT LEVEL SKILLS

The Speed Demon

- Master the crossover step
- Perfect your acceleration
- Learn to read pitchers' moves (see below)

Learning Pitchers' Moves: Become a Base-Stealing Detective!

When you're on base, turn into a super-spy watching the pitcher's every move!

Study their feet like a detective with a magnifying glass. Does the pitcher lift the front foot first when throwing home? That's your GREEN LIGHT to steal! But if they lift that back leg first, FREEZE - they're probably throwing to your base!

Count how long the pitcher holds the ball before throwing. One-Mississippi, Two-Mississippi... If it's always the same count, you can time your jump perfectly!

Notice tiny clues: a glance over the shoulder, a special grip, or tense shoulders. These "tells" are like the pitcher accidentally showing their secret cards!

The best base stealers aren't just speedy - they're master detectives who crack the pitcher's secret code! Watch, learn, and then ZOOM to the next base when they least expect it!

The Slide Specialist

- Practice pop-up slides
- Master the hook slide (see below)
- Perfect the head-first slide (with coach's permission!)

Mastering the Hook Slide

When that play at second base is going to be CLOSE, it's time to unleash your HOOK SLIDE magic! This isn't your ordinary straight-in slide - it's your ninja move to avoid the tag!

As you blast toward the base, start your slide a little EARLIER than normal. Then, instead of sliding straight, swing your legs AWAY from the base in a big "J" shape! Your foot hooks around to catch just the corner of the bag while your body curves AWAY from where the fielder is trying to tag you!

The secret to a perfect hook slide? Keep your arms UP and away from the dirt! One arm points to the sky like you're reaching for a star, while your other arm is ready to grab the base. This keeps your fingers safe from cleats and makes you a smaller target!

Practice makes perfect! Start by hook sliding on grass until you get the feel for it. Soon you'll be curving around tags like a slippery fish, making highlight-reel slides that leave fielders swiping at nothing but air! Remember - in baseball, it's not just about being FAST, it's about being SNEAKY too!

The Base Path Brain

- Study pitcher tendencies
- Learn to read pickoff moves
- Master situational running (see below)

Mastering Situational Running: Smart Baserunners Win!

Being a great baserunner isn't just about speed - it's about making the RIGHT move at the RIGHT time!

With less than two outs and a fly ball, FREEZE until you see it land! Tag up if it's caught, but ZOOM if it drops! Like a superhero knowing when to use their special powers.

When you're on first base and your teammate hits a ground ball, BLAST off to second! Break up the double play like you're splitting atoms - this helps your team even if YOU get out!

Running with two outs? GO GO GO on contact! But with nobody out, be careful like a treasure hunter - sometimes staying safe is smarter than risking it all.

Remember the scoreboard is your secret map! Tie game? Be bold! Big lead? Play it safe! The smartest baserunners aren't just fast with their feet - they're quick with their brains!**Pro Secret!** Some MLB players practice sliding on wet tarps during rain delays! (Don't try this without permission!)

Warning! Speed is awesome, but smart running wins games. Don't be fast and foolish!

More Fun Facts!

- Amazing!: The longest rundown in MLB history lasted 29 seconds!
- Wild Stuff: Some players can steal bases without sliding!
- Cool Beans: Base stealers study over 100 different pickoff moves!

P.S. If anyone asks why you're practicing slides in your backyard, tell them you're "analyzing friction coefficients through controlled deceleration experiments." Then steal their base while they're trying to figure that out!

Remember: Great base runners aren't born - they're made one slide at a time! Keep running, future speedster!

Chapter 9

Practice Like a Pro (Train Like a Pro, Live Like a Kid)

Let's be honest - practice isn't always as exciting as game day. Maybe you've been swinging at the same tee for what feels like centuries, or throwing into a net until your arm feels like spaghetti. Sometimes you might wonder if all those repetitions really matter (spoiler alert: they do!).

Right now, you might be the player who counts down the minutes until practice is over, or maybe you're already the first one there and last one to leave. Either way, what you do when nobody's watching is what makes you amazing when everyone is watching. Even if your current practice routine involves mostly trying not to hit yourself with the ball.

It's time to turn those boring practice sessions into your secret superpower! Because while talent might make you good, it's practice that makes you great. And hey, at least you don't have to practice like Ted Williams - he used to swing a bat in front of a mirror for hours (though we know you've tried that too!).

Fun Facts That'll Blow Your Mind!

- Did you know? MLB players take about 500 practice swings per day!
- Wow Factor: Pitchers throw over 100 practice pitches between starts!
- Mind Blown: Players practice fielding over 100 ground balls daily!
- Super Cool: Some pros practice for 6 hours before a 3-hour game!

Team Player Tale: Tony Gwynn's Swing Science

Meet Tony Gwynn, the guy who turned batting practice into a science! Back when most players were just swinging away, Tony was filming every single one of his at-bats (way before TikTok was cool). He'd study these videos for hours, learning exactly how to perfect his swing. The result? He hit .338 for his career - that's like getting a hit every third time up! He was so good at practicing, other players started copying him. Now that's what we call a trendsetter!

Practice Like You Mean It

The Perfect Practice Plan:

- Start with a warm-up (no cold muscles allowed!)
- Mix up your drills (boring practice = boring results)
- Focus on form (then speed it up)
- Track your progress (celebrate the small wins!)

Emergency Situations!

When Practice Gets Boring:

- Create a game out of it
- Challenge yourself

- Set mini-goals
- Remember why you started

When You're Not Seeing Results:

- Stay patient (Rome wasn't built in a batting practice)
- Focus on small improvements
- Ask for help
- Keep grinding!

NEXT LEVEL SKILLS

The Practice Pro

- Create your own drills
- Design skill challenges
- Make practice fun for others

The Self-Coach

- Film your mechanics
- Study your form
- Learn to self-correct

The Drill Master

- Combine multiple skills
- Practice game situations
- Create pressure scenarios (see below)

Create Practice Scenarios: Be Your Own Baseball Gamemaster!

Why just practice boring old drills when you can create REAL GAME situations that get your heart pounding? Turn practice into your own baseball adventure game!

Grab your teammates and shout, "Runners on first and third, one out, we're down by one run in the FINAL INNING!" Suddenly, that routine ground ball isn't so routine anymore! The fielder feels the pressure, the runners get realistic practice, and EVERYONE learns how to handle game-time stress!

Pitchers, set up count scenarios! "It's 3-2 with bases loaded!" Now that pitch matters WAY more than just throwing strikes. Batters, give yourself tough situations too - "Two strikes, runner on second, gotta move him over!" Your brain learns to handle pressure when you PRACTICE with pressure!

The best teams don't just practice skills - they practice SITUATIONS! Add imaginary scores, counts, and runners to every drill. Make up wild scenarios like, "There's a zombie on first base and he steals on EVERY pitch!" (Okay, maybe not that one...) But the more game-like your practice, the more your real games will feel like just another practice! Soon you'll be the clutch player who stays cool when everyone else panics!

Pro Secret! Some MLB players practice with smaller equipment to make the real game feel easier!

Warning! Practice makes permanent - so practice the right way!

More Fun Facts!

- Amazing!: Players can swing a bat over 2,000 times in one practice session!
- Wild Stuff: Some teams practice at midnight to beat the heat!
- Cool Beans: Fielders catch over 200 flies in practice each day!

P.S. If anyone asks why you're practicing so much, tell them you're "implementing systematic performance enhancement protocols through repetitive kinesthetic engagement." Then show them your awesome new skills while they're still confused!

Remember: Practice doesn't make perfect - perfect practice makes perfect! Keep working, future star!

Chapter 10

The Extra Special Stuff (All the Cool Things That Don't Fit Anywhere Else!)

Welcome to the bonus round, MVP! This is where we cover all the cool stuff that doesn't fit anywhere else - the secret tips, the ninja moves, and yes, even how to get bubble gum out of your cap (it happens to the best of us).

Maybe you're already mastering the basics and ready for some advanced tricks, or maybe you just want to learn how to look cool while waiting for your skills to catch up. Either way, this chapter is packed with the kind of baseball magic that turns good players into legends (and regular gum-chewers into bubble-blowing artists).

Think of this as your baseball swiss army knife - full of tools you might not need every day, but when you do need them, you'll be glad you learned them. From rain delays to rally caps, from superstitions to celebrations, we're about to turn you into a complete baseball player. Just remember - with great power comes great responsibility (and usually some grass stains).

Fun Facts That'll Blow Your Mind!

- Did you know? Some MLB teams have over 50 different celebrations!
- Wow Factor: Players can communicate using more than 100 secret signals!
- Mind Blown: Teams have special plays just for trick situations!
- Super Cool: Some stadiums have secret passages under the dugouts!

Special Situation Success

The Weather Warrior:

- Playing in the rain (without slipping)
- Handling the wind (it's not always your friend)
- Beating the heat (without melting)
- Cold weather tricks (keep those hands warm!)

The Equipment Expert:

- Break in your glove properly
- Take care of your bat
- Keep your cleats game-ready
- Pack your bag like a pro (see below)

Pack Your Bag Like a Pro: Your Baseball Command Center!

Every baseball superhero needs their special gear ready for action! Packing your bag isn't just about remembering stuff - it's about being PREPARED for anything the game throws at you!

Start with your BASEBALL HEADQUARTERS - a good bat bag with separate compartments. Bats go in the special slots (not rattling around with everything else!), helmet gets its own space, and your lucky glove deserves the premium spot where it won't get squished!

Don't forget your SECRET WEAPONS: extra batting gloves (they always disappear!), a backup pair of socks (puddles happen!), sunscreen for day games, and maybe a special snack for between-inning energy boosts! Pack a water bottle that won't leak all over your gear - nothing worse than soggy batting gloves!

The REAL pros always bring extras to share - some tape, a few Band-Aids, or a spare pencil for scoring. Your teammates will think you're a GENIUS when you save the day with that extra hair tie or batting doughnut! Remember, the best players aren't just prepared for themselves - they're ready to help the whole team shine!

Emergency Situations!

When Things Get Weird:

- Ball hits a bird (yes, it's happened!)
- Uniform malfunctions
- Equipment breaks
- Strange rules come up

When You Need to Improvise:

- Missing equipment
- Unexpected position changes (see below)

- Surprise situations
- Emergency backup plans

Unexpected Position Changes: Your Baseball Adventure Quest!

Your coach yells, " You're playing THIRD BASE this inning!" – but you've NEVER played third before! Don't panic! Baseball loves to throw curveballs at you, and not just from the pitcher's mound!

Think of surprise position changes as your chance to become a baseball SUPERHERO! Normally an outfielder? Now you get to vacuum up grounders like a human dirt devil! Usually play first base? Suddenly you're behind the plate catching fireballs! Each new position teaches your baseball brain something AMAZING that makes you better everywhere else!

The secret weapon for handling position switches? SPEAK UP and ASK QUESTIONS! "Coach, where should I play for a lefty batter?" or "Should I cover second on steals?" Your teammates will help too - they'd rather answer your questions than watch you stand in the wrong spot! Remember, the most VALUABLE players on any team are the ones who can play anywhere and be ready for anything! So next time coach sends you to a new spot, smile big and think, "Time for my next baseball adventure!"

NEXT LEVEL SKILLS

The Trick Play Master

- Hidden ball tricks

- Fake throws
- Delayed steals
- Special signals (see below)

Baseball's Secret Signals: The Hidden Language!

Watch closely - baseball has its own secret code language that only team members understand!

See the coach touching his cap, then his nose, then tugging his ear? That's not an itchy day - he's sending a SECRET MESSAGE to the batter! Maybe it means "Bunt now!" or "Watch for a steal!"

Catchers have magic finger signals too! One finger for fastball, two for curve, and special wiggles for special pitches. It's like spy talk that tells the pitcher exactly what to throw!

Even players share secret signs! A shortstop might tap his chest to tell the second baseman, "I'll cover the bag on this play!" All without saying a single word!

Learning these baseball signals is like joining a super-secret club. The other team is trying to crack your code, so teams change their signals often. Pay attention, and soon you'll be reading the secret language of baseball like a pro

The Celebration Creator

- Team victory moves
- Personal success celebrations

- Dugout routines
- Rally starters (see below)

Rally Starters: How to Spark Baseball Magic!

When your team needs runs, it's time to become a RALLY STARTER and light the baseball magic fire!

A simple walk can be the spark! Work the count, be patient like a cat waiting to pounce. Drawing a walk might seem boring, but it's like lighting the fuse on a fireworks show - what comes next is EXPLOSIVE!

Hit behind the runner? That's rally science! A ground ball through the spot the second baseman just left feels like you've discovered a secret passage. Your coach will think you're a baseball genius!

Never give up on infield hits! Sprint like your shoes are rocket-powered, even on routine grounders. That hustle might force a rushed throw, and BOOM - you're safe and the rally keeps growing!

The best rally starters don't need home runs - they're masters of "just enough" hits that keep the line moving. A bloop here, a seeing-eye single there, and suddenly the scoreboard is lighting up like a pinball machine! Remember, big innings often start with the smallest spark!

The Situation Specialist

- Weird play knowledge (see below)
- Emergency position skills

- Backup plans for everything

Weird Play Knowledge: Baseball's Strangest Superpowers!

Baseball isn't just about the normal stuff - it's packed with BIZARRE situations that happen once in a blue moon, and knowing these weird rules makes you look like a BASEBALL GENIUS!

Did you know if a batted ball gets STUCK in a player's jersey or equipment, the batter gets TWO bases? Or that if a ball bounces off a bird (yes, a BIRD!) in mid-air, it's still in play?! What about the hidden ball trick, where an infielder pretends to throw the ball back to the pitcher but secretly keeps it to tag a runner who steps off the base? SNEAKY!

The strangest rules are the most fun! If you hit a home run but miss touching home plate, the other team can APPEAL, and you're out! Or if two runners end up on the same base, the defense can tag EITHER one! Knowing these odd situations is like having baseball superpowers - while everyone else stands around confused, YOU'LL be the one explaining what just happened! So learn the weird plays, and next time baseball gets CRAZY, you'll be the smartest kid on the field!

Pro Secret! Some MLB teams practice crazy situations just once a year - but when they need them, they're ready!

Warning! Cool tricks are fun, but fundamentals win games. Master the basics first

Cool Story: The Kid Who Could See The Spin

Before he was "The Kid," Ken Griffey Jr. was just a 10-year-old boy with the

WEIRDEST baseball habit anyone had ever seen. While other kids would swing at anything near the plate, little Ken would stand perfectly still, watching pitches zoom by.

"What are you DOING?" his coach would yell. "SWING THE BAT!"

But Ken had a secret superpower nobody knew about. While everyone else just saw a white blur, Ken could actually SEE the red seams SPINNING on the baseball! He'd watch closely, noticing how curveballs spun one way and fastballs another. His eyes were like super-slow-motion cameras!

One day at Little League, the opposing team had a pitcher who threw so hard that parents whispered he was too dangerous to face. Kids were stepping out of the batter's box before the pitch even arrived! But when it was Ken's turn, he stepped right in without fear.

The first pitch came ZOOMING in like a rocket! Ken didn't even flinch - he just watched those red seams spinning. "STRIKE ONE!" yelled the umpire. The second pitch - even FASTER - same result. The crowd held their breath for strike three.

But Ken had seen enough. He knew EXACTLY how the ball was spinning now. When the third pitch came, his bat FLASHED through the air with that sweet, smooth swing that would someday become famous. CRACK! The ball soared over the fence, over the trees, and landed in a creek beyond the park!

Years later, when Ken Griffey Jr. was crushing home runs in the Major Leagues with the most beautiful swing baseball had ever seen, reporters would ask how he made it look so easy. He'd just smile and say, "I can see things other people can't." And he wasn't kidding - he really could see the seams spin!

More Fun Facts!

- Amazing!: There are over 200 different baseball superstitions!
- Wild Stuff: Some players have never stepped on a foul line... ever!
- Cool Beans: Teams have plays for when the lights go out!

P.S. If anyone asks why you're practicing weird plays, tell them you're "preparing for statistically improbable yet potentially decisive game-altering scenarios." Then do something awesome while they're trying to figure out what you said!

Remember: Baseball is a game of surprises - be ready for anything! Keep learning, future legend!

Chapter 11

You're On Your Way to Baseball Stardom! (And Maybe, Those Grass Stains Will Eventually Come Out)

Take a deep breath, baseball star. Feel that? That's the feeling of accomplishment. Whether you've read this book cover to cover in one day (we see you, super fan!), or you've been taking it one chapter at a time between practices, you've already shown the dedication it takes to be great.

Remember that first day you picked up this book? Maybe your throws were a bit wild (okay, very wild), your catches were more like adventures, and your batting stance made your coach scratch their head. But you didn't give up. You kept reading, kept learning, and most importantly, kept trying.

Think about all those practice sessions in your backyard. The times you threw the ball over the fence (sorry, neighbors!). The makeshift batting practice with rolled-up socks when it was raining. The countless times you practiced your victory celebration in front of the mirror (don't worry, we won't tell anyone about the dance moves).

You've probably discovered by now that baseball isn't just about physical skills - it's about heart, determination, and the willingness to look a little silly sometimes while you're learning. Every MLB star was once a kid just like you, probably getting hit in the shin with ground balls and accidentally throwing their bat farther than they hit the ball.

Sure, you might still miss a few catches, and maybe your throws occasionally end up in interesting places. Perhaps you're still working on hitting the ball more often than you hit air. But guess what? That's exactly where you're supposed to be right now. Baseball isn't about being perfect - it's about getting better every single day.

Think about it: Even the greatest players in baseball history had to learn the basics. Babe Ruth probably dropped easy fly balls. Mickey Mantle probably tripped running to first base. Ken Griffey Jr. probably had days where he couldn't hit the broad side of a barn. But they kept going, kept practicing, and kept believing in themselves.

And now here you are, armed with knowledge about everything from throwing techniques to dugout etiquette, from batting stances to baseball brains. You've learned about being a great teammate, handling pressure, and even what to do when everything goes wrong (which, let's face it, happens to everyone sometimes).

But here's the really cool part - your baseball journey is just beginning! Whether you dream of playing in the World Series or just want to be the best player you can be, you've already taken the most important step: deciding to learn and improve. Every great baseball story starts with a kid who's willing to put in the work, face their fears, and maybe get a few grass stains along the way.

What You've Learned:

- How to throw without hitting innocent bystanders
- Ways to catch balls (instead of wearing them)
- The art of hitting (making contact is way better than creating a breeze)
- Fielding skills that make ground balls less scary
- Base running that doesn't look like you're lost

- How to be the teammate everyone high-fives
- And so much more!

Fun Final Facts!

- Did you know? Every MLB star started as a kid just like you!
- Wow Factor: Most pros struck out hundreds of times before making it big!
- Mind Blown: Even Hall of Famers had coaches tell them to "keep practicing"!
- Super Cool: The best players never stop learning new things!

Remember These Golden Rules:

- Everyone starts somewhere (usually missing the ball completely)
- Practice makes progress (perfect comes later)
- Having fun is part of getting better
- The best players are always good teammates
- It's okay to make mistakes (that's how you learn!)

Your Next Steps:

1. Keep practicing (but don't forget to have fun)

2. Help others learn (sharing knowledge makes you better)

3. Stay positive (even when you hit yourself with the bat)

4. Never stop believing in yourself

One Last Pro Secret!

Even the biggest stars in baseball still work on the basics every single day. They just make it look easier (and probably have fewer grass stains).

Final Words of Wisdom

Baseball is an amazing game that can teach you so much - about sports, about life, and about yourself. Whether you end up playing in the World Series or just having a blast with your friends, the skills and lessons you've learned here will help you succeed both on and off the field.

P.S. If anyone asks what you learned from this book, tell them you've mastered "advanced kinesthetic spatial awareness through spherical projectile manipulation." Or just show them your awesome new skills - that works too!

Keep this book handy - you never know when you'll need to refresh your memory on becoming totally awesome at baseball!

Remember: The most important stat in baseball isn't batting average, home runs, or strikeouts - it's how much heart you put into the game!

See you on the diamond, superstar!

Chapter 12

Inspirational Stories: Baseball Legends Who Changed the Game

Babe Ruth: The Orphan Who Became Baseball's First Superstar

On a cold February day in 1914, a nineteen-year-old pitcher with an awkward delivery and unusual mannerisms stood nervously on a baseball field in Fayetteville, North Carolina. The minor league Baltimore Orioles were conducting spring training, and the young left-hander was about to face his first professional batter. Team veterans watched skeptically as the ungainly teenager wound up and delivered his first pitch.

What happened next would begin one of the most extraordinary stories in sports history.

George Herman "Babe" Ruth Jr. wasn't supposed to become an American legend. Born in 1895 to working-class parents in Baltimore, his childhood was marked by neglect and hardship. His father, George Sr., ran a saloon and spent little time with his son. His mother, Kate, suffered from poor health throughout Babe's early years.

By his own admission, young George was a troublemaker. "I was a bad kid,"

Ruth later recalled. "I didn't mean to cause trouble, but there was something in me. I just couldn't stand still."

At age seven, his parents, unable to control him and struggling financially, made the difficult decision to send him to St. Mary's Industrial School for Boys, a combination orphanage and reform school. The moment would have broken many children, but it ultimately proved to be Babe's salvation.

"It was at St. Mary's that I first began to realize the world wasn't so bad," Ruth later wrote. "I learned discipline, faith, and the value of hard work."

The most significant influence in Ruth's life at St. Mary's was Brother Matthias Boutlier, a disciplinarian with a soft spot for baseball. The imposing Catholic brother introduced Ruth to the game, teaching him fundamentals during recreation periods. Ruth showed natural ability, and Brother Matthias gave him extra attention, molding not just his baseball skills but his character.

"He taught me to read and write and encouraged my baseball," Ruth said of Brother Matthias. "He was the father I needed and the model I lacked."

Ruth rarely left St. Mary's during his formative years, spending nearly twelve years at the institution. Rather than growing resentful, he threw himself into baseball, developing the powerful swing that would later revolutionize the game. Brother Matthias's influence remained so important that years later, at the height of his fame, Ruth would often return to visit his mentor.

In February 1914, Jack Dunn, owner of the Baltimore Orioles (then a minor league team), visited St. Mary's to scout the talented young pitcher. Impressed with what he saw, Dunn arranged to become Ruth's legal guardian so the nineteen-year-old could sign a professional contract. When Ruth arrived at training camp, older players dubbed him "Jack Dunn's baby"—soon shortened to "Babe," a nickname that would stick for life.

Ruth's pitching abilities quickly became apparent. His unique left-handed delivery and devastating fastball overwhelmed minor league hitters. By July, the struggling Orioles, facing financial difficulties, sold Ruth's contract to the Boston Red Sox. By the end of the season, the former reform school student was pitching in the major leagues.

As a pitcher for Boston from 1914 to 1919, Ruth was exceptional, winning 89 games and posting a remarkable 2.19 ERA. He helped the Red Sox win three World Series titles during this period. But Ruth's greatest contribution to baseball history was yet to come.

Unlike most pitchers of his era (or any era), Ruth could hit with extraordinary power. As the Red Sox began playing him in the outfield between pitching starts to keep his bat in the lineup, Ruth discovered his true calling. In 1919, while still occasionally pitching, he hit 29 home runs—a stunning total that broke the previous single-season record of 27.

Then came the moment that would change baseball forever and create one of sports' most enduring curses. Red Sox owner Harry Frazee, facing financial difficulties, sold Ruth's contract to the rival New York Yankees for $100,000 (over $1.5 million in today's money) plus a loan. The transaction would haunt Boston for 86 years as the "Curse of the Bambino."

In New York, freed from pitching duties and playing in a stadium that would soon be nicknamed "The House That Ruth Built," Babe revolutionized baseball with his unprecedented power. In 1920, his first full season with the Yankees, Ruth hit 54 home runs—more than any entire team that year except the Philadelphia Phillies.

The following year, he hit 59 homers, a record that would stand until he himself broke it with 60 in 1927. These weren't just incremental improvements to existing records; they represented a fundamental shift in how baseball was played. Ruth's power-hitting approach transformed a game previously built around singles, stolen bases, and sacrifice bunts into the more dynamic, home run-centric sport we recognize today.

But Ruth's impact extended far beyond his statistical achievements. The 1920s—often called "The Roaring Twenties"—saw America embracing a new, more exuberant cultural identity after the hardships of World War I. Ruth, with his larger-than-life personality, embodied this new spirit. While previous baseball stars had often been reserved and businesslike, Ruth was boisterous, charismatic, and unashamedly fun-loving.

"He wasn't just a baseball player," historian Doris Kearns Goodwin noted. "He was the dawn of a new era. He created the modern concept of a sports celebrity."

Ruth's impact on baseball's popularity was immense. Before his arrival, baseball was recovering from the 1919 "Black Sox" scandal, when eight Chicago White Sox players were accused of intentionally losing the World Series. Ruth's exciting play and magnetic personality helped restore public faith in the game. Attendance at Yankee games doubled, and other teams saw their crowds grow when the Yankees came to town. Everyone wanted to see the "Sultan of Swat."

Yet Ruth's mammoth success was not without personal challenges. His appetites—for food, alcohol, and women—were as outsized as his baseball achievements. Despite marrying Helen Woodford in 1914, Ruth was notorious for his womanizing. His drinking and late-night carousing frequently frustrated his managers and teammates.

These behaviors stemmed partly from Ruth's difficult childhood and the sudden wealth and fame he acquired. "I grew up in reform school," he once explained. "I never had any money, and then suddenly I had more than I could ever spend. What would you have done?"

Despite these excesses, Ruth maintained a remarkable connection with children. Having grown up essentially as an orphan, he had immense sympathy for disadvantaged youth. He regularly visited children's hospitals and orphanages, often without publicity. In one famous story, he promised a seriously ill boy, Johnny Sylvester, that he would hit a home run for him in the 1926 World Series—then proceeded to hit three.

Ruth's relationship with teammates was complex. His salary—$80,000 in 1930, more than President Herbert Hoover earned—created some resentment. When asked why he deserved more money than the President, Ruth famously quipped, "I had a better year than he did." Yet many teammates respected his unmatched work ethic in practice and his ability to perform under pressure.

As the 1920s gave way to the 1930s, even Ruth couldn't escape the effects of age. His numbers declined gradually, and by 1934, the Yankees decided to release him. He finished his career with short stints for the Boston Braves and Brooklyn Dodgers, officially retiring in 1935 with 714 career home runs, a record that would stand for nearly 40 years.

Ruth desperately wanted to manage after his playing career ended, but no offers came. Team owners, perhaps wary of his sometimes wild behavior, repeatedly passed him over. This rejection deeply hurt Ruth, who believed his baseball knowledge and leadership abilities were underestimated.

In his post-playing years, Ruth matured. After Helen's death in a house fire, he married Claire Hodgson in 1929, and her stabilizing influence helped him become more disciplined. He reduced his drinking, lost weight, and devoted more time to charitable causes, particularly those benefiting children.

In 1946, Ruth was diagnosed with nasopharyngeal cancer. Despite numerous treatments, his health declined rapidly. On June 13, 1948, he made his final public appearance at Yankee Stadium for the retirement of his number 3, appearing gaunt and using a bat as a cane. In his speech that day, his voice hoarse from radiation treatments, Ruth addressed the capacity crowd as "the only real people I've ever known."

Two months later, on August 16, 1948, Ruth died at age 53. His body lay in state at Yankee Stadium, where an estimated 77,000 people filed past to pay respects. Over 75,000 mourners stood outside St. Patrick's Cathedral during his funeral. For a man born to indifferent parents and raised in a reform school, it was an extraordinary outpouring of public grief.

Ruth's baseball statistics remain astonishing even by modern standards. His career slugging percentage of .690 still ranks highest all-time. His 714 home runs stood as the record until Hank Aaron surpassed it in 1974. Perhaps most remarkably, Ruth hit more home runs by himself than entire teams did regularly during his era.

But Ruth's legacy transcends numbers. As the first true sports superstar of the modern media age, he transformed how Americans viewed athletes. Before Ruth, sports figures were admired primarily for their athletic prowess and often expected to maintain a modest public persona. Ruth introduced the concept of the athlete as entertainer and cultural icon.

For young baseball players today, Ruth's story offers timeless inspiration. His rise from a troubled childhood in a reform school to the pinnacle of American sports demonstrates the power of natural talent developed through dedicated practice. His ability to reinvent himself—from dominant pitcher to revolutionary slugger—showcases the importance of adaptability and willingness to evolve.

Perhaps most importantly, Ruth never forgot his own difficult beginnings. Despite his fame and fortune, he maintained a special connection with disadvantaged children throughout his life. When asked about his generous charitable work, particularly with children, Ruth explained simply: "I was one of them."

The boy who once seemed destined for obscurity instead became one of America's most enduring cultural figures—the Sultan of Swat, the Bambino, the home run king who forever changed baseball and defined the modern sports hero. In the words sportswriter Jimmy Cannon famously wrote: "Babe Ruth wasn't a baseball player. He was a worldwide disaster... an eruption of the national joy."

From St. Mary's Industrial School to Yankee Stadium, George Herman Ruth's improbable journey reminds us that greatness can emerge from the most unlikely beginnings—and that sometimes, the most powerful swing can come from the hands that once had nothing at all.

Jackie Robinson: Breaking Barriers with Courage and Grace

On April 15, 1947, a 28-year-old rookie stepped onto Ebbets Field in Brooklyn wearing the number 42, marking a moment that would forever change not just baseball, but America itself. As Jack Roosevelt Robinson took his position at first base for the Brooklyn Dodgers, he wasn't just playing a game—he was challenging nearly sixty years of rigid segregation in America's national pastime.

The weight on his shoulders that day was almost unimaginable. Every move, every reaction, every performance would be scrutinized not just as the actions of one player, but as a referendum on whether Black Americans belonged in Major League Baseball. Yet somehow, amid death threats, vicious racial taunts, and isolation from teammates, Jackie Robinson performed with a combination of athletic brilliance and personal dignity that would eventually transform a sport and help advance a civil rights movement.

Born on January 31, 1919, in Cairo, Georgia, Robinson's early years offered little hint of his future historical significance. He was the youngest of five children born to Jerry and Mallie Robinson, sharecroppers who struggled against the oppressive racial dynamics of the rural South. When Jackie was just an infant, his father abandoned the family, forcing Mallie to seek better opportunities in California.

The Robinson family settled in Pasadena, where they faced different but still significant racial barriers. Despite California's reputation for greater tolerance, the Robinsons encountered housing discrimination and social exclusion. These early experiences with injustice helped shape Jackie's character and his eventual willingness to challenge unfair systems.

Athletics provided Robinson's first avenue for distinguishing himself. At John Muir High School and later Pasadena Junior College, he excelled in multiple sports, including football, basketball, track, and baseball. His extraordinary versatility eventually earned him a place at UCLA, where he became the first athlete in school history to letter in four sports. Remarkably, baseball—the sport that would make him immortal—might have been his fourth-best sport at the time.

"He was the best all-around athlete I've ever seen," recalled UCLA football coach Babe Horrell. "He could have been All-American in any of three sports."

Robinson's athletic career was interrupted by World War II when he was drafted into the U.S. Army in 1942. Even in military service, Robinson refused to accept discrimination silently. When ordered to move to the back of a segregated military bus at Fort Hood, Texas, Robinson declined. The resulting confrontation led to a court-martial, though Robinson was ultimately acquitted of all charges.

This incident demonstrated a quality that would define Robinson's approach to injustice—a willingness to stand his ground against discrimination, even at personal risk. It also caught the attention of a baseball executive who was quietly planning to challenge baseball's color barrier.

Branch Rickey, president and general manager of the Brooklyn Dodgers, had been searching for the right player to integrate baseball. He needed someone with not just exceptional athletic ability, but the strength of character to withstand the inevitable backlash. In Robinson, he found his candidate.

Their first meeting in August 1945 has become legendary. Rickey subjected Robinson to a three-hour interview, during which he role-played various scenarios of racial abuse Robinson would likely face—fans shouting slurs, pitchers throwing at his head, hotels refusing service, teammates shunning him.

"I'm looking for a ballplayer with guts enough not to fight back," Rickey told him, explaining that responding to provocations would only reinforce stereotypes and give segregationists ammunition.

Robinson famously asked, "Mr. Rickey, are you looking for a Negro who is afraid to fight back?"

"No," Rickey responded, "I need a player with guts enough not to fight back."

Robinson agreed to this extraordinary demand: he would turn the other cheek for his first two seasons, despite his natural competitive fire and commitment to standing up for himself. It was a strategic decision that required immense self-control.

Robinson's journey to the majors began with the Montreal Royals, the Dodgers' top minor league affiliate, in 1946. Despite tremendous pressure, he excelled, winning the International League batting title with a .349 average and leading Montreal to a championship. His success in Montreal, where Canadian fans proved more welcoming than many American crowds would be, convinced Rickey that Robinson was ready for the ultimate test.

When Robinson made his major league debut on April 15, 1947, he broke a color barrier that had stood since the 1880s, when the last Black players were forced out of organized baseball. The response was immediate and often cruel. Some Dodger teammates initially circulated a petition refusing to play with him. Opposing players hurled racial slurs, and pitchers targeted him with beanballs. Hotels and restaurants refused service to the entire team rather than accommodate Robinson.

The abuse reached its peak during a May series in Cincinnati, where Reds players and fans subjected Robinson to particularly vicious harassment. Dodger shortstop Pee Wee Reese, a white Southerner, responded with a simple but powerful gesture, walking across the infield to put his arm around Robinson's shoulders—a public show of support that silenced the crowd and became an iconic moment in the story of baseball's integration.

Through it all, Robinson maintained the composure he had promised Rickey, channeling his frustration into his play. He finished his rookie season with a .297 batting average, led the league in stolen bases, and won the inaugural Major League Baseball Rookie of the Year Award. The Dodgers won the National League pennant, though they fell to the Yankees in the World Series.

By 1949, Robinson was freed from his promise to turn the other cheek, and his natural competitiveness emerged more fully. He won the National League MVP award that year, batting .342 with 124 RBIs and 37 stolen bases. His aggressive baserunning style and ability to disrupt pitchers' concentration became hallmarks of his play.

"Robinson could hit and bunt and steal and run. He had intimidation on his side and he burned with a dark fire," wrote Roger Kahn in "The Boys of Summer." "He wanted passionately to win. He bore the burden of a pioneer and the weight made him stronger."

Beyond his statistical achievements, Robinson changed how baseball was played. His aggressive baserunning, described by sportswriter Red Smith as "taking a lead off first with the dynamics of a coiled spring," forced opponents to adapt to a style of play they'd rarely encountered. Modern fans watching Robinson's highlight films are struck by how contemporary his play appears—he was, in many ways, ahead of his time.

Robinson's courage created opportunities for other Black players. By the end of 1947, four more had joined major league teams. Larry Doby integrated the American League with the Cleveland Indians just months after Robinson's debut. The great Satchel Paige, after decades dominating the Negro Leagues, finally got his chance at the majors at age 42.

Despite his on-field success, Robinson's personal experience remained challenging. Road trips meant enduring segregated facilities throughout much of the country. Death threats were common enough that the FBI maintained a file on potential dangers to Robinson. Through these trials, his wife Rachel provided crucial support, becoming his confidant and emotional anchor.

"I never had it made," Robinson would later write, correcting those who assumed his wealth and fame insulated him from racism's effects.

Robinson played ten seasons with the Dodgers, helping the team to six National League pennants and a World Championship in 1955. When he retired after the 1956 season, his career batting average stood at .311, and he had been selected for six consecutive All-Star games. The Dodgers traded him to the New York Giants after his final season, but Robinson chose retirement instead, partly due to his previously undisclosed struggles with diabetes.

His post-baseball life was marked by continued civil rights activism. He became an executive at Chock Full o'Nuts coffee company—another racial barrier broken—and was active in the NAACP and other civil rights organizations. He corresponded with presidents and testified before Congress on civil rights issues. Though his health declined prematurely due to diabetes complications, his voice remained powerful in the fight for equality.

Robinson's later years brought both recognition and disappointment. He became the first Black player inducted into the Baseball Hall of Fame in 1962, receiving 77.5% of the vote in his first year of eligibility. Yet he grew increasingly impatient with the pace of progress in baseball, criticizing the sport for its slow advancement of Black managers and executives.

His final public appearance came at the 1972 World Series, where he threw out the ceremonial first pitch commemorating the 25th anniversary of his breaking the color barrier. In his speech that day, just nine days before his death at age 53, Robinson acknowledged progress but pushed for more: "I'm going to be tremendously more pleased and more proud when I look at that third base coaching line and see a black face managing in baseball."

Robinson died on October 24, 1972, having lived long enough to see his impact on the game but not long enough to see his final wish fulfilled. It would take another three years before Frank Robinson (no relation) became MLB's first Black manager with the Cleveland Indians in 1975.

In 1997, on the 50th anniversary of Robinson's debut, Major League Baseball took the unprecedented step of retiring his number 42 across all teams, the only player in MLB history accorded this honor. Each year on April 15, now known as "Jackie Robinson Day," every player on every team wears number 42 to commemorate his legacy.

For young ballplayers, Robinson's journey offers profound lessons that transcend sports. His story demonstrates how athletic excellence can be a platform for social change when coupled with exceptional character. His willingness to endure abuse without retaliation for a greater cause illustrates that sometimes restraint requires more courage than confrontation.

Perhaps the most powerful aspect of Robinson's legacy is how he balanced uncompromising determination with strategic flexibility. While he never accepted the fundamental injustice of racism, he tactically chose when and how to fight it, understanding that how one challenges a system can be as important as the challenge itself.

As Robinson himself wrote in his autobiography: "A life is not important except in the impact it has on other lives." By that measure, few baseball players—few Americans of any profession—have lived more important lives than Jackie Robinson. The barriers he broke extended far beyond the baselines of

Ebbets Field, helping to inspire and accelerate a civil rights movement that would fundamentally reshape American society.

From sharecropper's son to American icon, Jackie Robinson's journey reminds us that courage doesn't always roar. Sometimes, it's the quiet dignity of a man who, with each step onto a baseball diamond, moved a nation closer to its professed ideals of freedom and equality for all.

Roberto Clemente: The Pride of Puerto Rico Who Died a Hero

On the shores of Carolina, Puerto Rico, a skinny boy with determined eyes would spend hours throwing rocks into the ocean, developing an arm that would one day astonish baseball fans across two continents. When he wasn't strengthening his arm, he was swinging tree branches at cans and stones, honing a batting style as unique as the path that lay before him.

Roberto Clemente Walker wasn't just practicing a game; he was preparing for a destiny that would make him not only one of baseball's greatest players but also its most profound humanitarian.

Born August 18, 1934, in Barrio San Antón, Carolina, Puerto Rico, Clemente was the youngest of seven children born to Luisa Walker and Melchor Clemente, a sugar cane worker who supplemented the family's modest income by working as a foreman and managing a small grocery store. Though poor by material standards, the Clemente household was rich in values that would shape Roberto's character—hard work, education, dignity, and compassion for others.

"My father taught me that work was a privilege, not an obligation," Clemente later said. "My mother taught me to give to others before thinking of myself."

From his earliest days, baseball was Clemente's passion. Without money for proper equipment, he improvised—milk cartons became gloves, broomsticks served as bats, and soup cans as balls. By his teen years, his extraordinary talent had become evident to local coaches. At 18, he joined the Santurce Crabbers of Puerto Rico's professional league, where he caught the attention of major league scouts.

The Brooklyn Dodgers signed Clemente to their minor league system in 1952, but they failed to protect him properly in the 1954 draft. The Pittsburgh Pirates, having finished last the previous season, had the first pick and selected Clemente, beginning a relationship that would define both his career and the franchise's history.

Arriving in Pittsburgh in 1955, the 20-year-old Clemente faced challenges that went beyond the playing field. He spoke limited English in an era when Latin American players were still relatively rare in the major leagues. He encountered prejudice both for his Hispanic heritage and his darker skin color. Reporters often mocked his accent in print, quoting him phonetically rather than correctly, and sometimes referred to him as "Bobby" despite his preference for Roberto.

These experiences with discrimination shaped Clemente's fierce pride in his Puerto Rican heritage and his determination to be treated with dignity. "I don't believe in color," he once stated firmly. "I believe in people. I am going to be judged by my name. My name is Roberto Clemente."

On the field, Clemente's unique style initially puzzled American baseball observers. He swung so hard he would often drop to one knee during his follow-through. His baserunning was aggressive to the point of appearing reckless. His throwing motion, developed on those Puerto Rican beaches, seemed almost casual until the ball arrived at its target with astonishing velocity and precision.

Pirates broadcaster Bob Prince captured Clemente's fielding prowess with a simple call whenever a ball was hit to right field: "Don't try it, he's got a rifle. He'll throw you out."

Despite hitting .255 as a rookie, Clemente's defensive skills and strong arm earned him regular playing time. By his third season, his batting average climbed to .311, and in 1960, he helped lead the Pirates to a dramatic World Series victory over the heavily favored New York Yankees. In the seven-game series, Clemente hit safely in every game, batting .310 while playing spectacular defense.

The following season, 1961, Clemente truly emerged as a superstar, winning the first of four batting titles with a .351 average. He would go on to win batting championships in 1964 (.339), 1965 (.329), and 1967 (.357), while developing power that would eventually produce 240 career home runs—an impressive total given the pitcher-friendly era and Pittsburgh's spacious Forbes Field.

Yet statistics alone fail to capture Clemente's brilliance. He played with an intensity and flair that reflected his belief that baseball was both art and competition. His contemporary Willie Stargell described watching Clemente play as "watching a kid at Christmas unwrapping a new toy."

Clemente's excellence was recognized with 12 consecutive Gold Glove awards (1961-1972) and 12 All-Star selections. In 1966, he was named National League MVP after batting .317 with 29 home runs and 119 RBIs. But the crowning achievement of his career came in 1971, when at age 37, he led the

Pirates to another World Series championship over the Baltimore Orioles.

In that series, Clemente delivered one of the greatest World Series performances in baseball history, hitting .414 with two home runs. After the Pirates' Game 7 victory, Clemente, selected as the World Series MVP, used his moment in the national spotlight to send a message. Speaking on national television, he first addressed his parents in Spanish—an unprecedented act at the time—saying: "Bendicion, Papi, Bendicion, Mami" ("Blessings, Father, Blessings, Mother").

This simple yet powerful gesture represented Clemente's unwavering commitment to his heritage at a time when Latin players were expected to assimilate and hide their cultural identity. "Why do I have to go to the back door?" he once asked. "Why can't I go around to the same door that the white boys enter?" For the increasing number of Latin American players in baseball, Clemente became both champion and voice.

Off the field, Clemente's humanitarian work became as legendary as his playing career. During offseasons, he conducted free baseball clinics for underprivileged children in Puerto Rico and other Latin American countries. He regularly visited hospitals and donated money to various causes without publicity. For Clemente, these weren't photo opportunities but moral obligations.

"Any time you have an opportunity to make a difference in this world and you don't, then you are wasting your time on Earth," he once said, a philosophy that would ultimately guide his final actions.

As Clemente approached his 3,000th hit—a milestone achieved by only 10 players before him—he remained focused on helping others. On September 30, 1972, he doubled off New York Mets left-hander Jon Matlack for hit number 3,000. None would have guessed it would be his last regular-season hit.

Three months later, on December 23, 1972, a devastating earthquake struck Managua, Nicaragua, killing thousands and leaving many more homeless. Clemente immediately organized relief efforts, collecting food, medicine, and clothing to be sent to the survivors. When he learned that three planeloads of supplies had been diverted by corrupt officials of the Somoza government, Clemente decided to accompany the fourth flight personally to ensure aid reached those in need.

On New Year's Eve 1972, despite warnings about the questionable condition of the chartered plane and its crew, Clemente boarded the overloaded DC-7 aircraft in San Juan. Shortly after takeoff, the plane experienced engine failure and crashed into the Atlantic Ocean. Clemente's body was never recovered.

The baseball world and beyond was stunned by the tragic loss. Clemente was just 38 years old, still an active player who had planned to continue his career in 1973. The Baseball Writers' Association of America held a special election to waive the standard five-year waiting period, and Clemente was inducted into the Hall of Fame in 1973.

Clemente's legacy extends far beyond his impressive statistics or even his cultural impact as a pioneer for Latin American players. His humanitarian spirit became institutionalized through the Roberto Clemente Award, given annually to the major league player who "best represents the game of baseball through extraordinary character, community involvement, philanthropy and positive contributions, both on and off the field."

In Puerto Rico, Clemente is revered not just as the island's greatest athlete but as its greatest ambassador. When Puerto Rico faced devastating Hurricane

Maria in 2017, relief workers reported finding Clemente's image displayed in homes that had lost everything else—a testament to his enduring symbolic power as a figure of hope and resilience.

For young players, especially those from Latin America and other underrepresented backgrounds, Clemente's journey offers profound inspiration. His insistence on being respected for both his play and his heritage established a model for athletes navigating cultural barriers. His commitment to excellence—he once said, "If you have a chance to accomplish something that will make things better for people coming behind you, and you don't do that, you are wasting your time on this earth"—set a standard for athletic achievement paired with social conscience.

Perhaps most powerfully, Clemente's life demonstrates how an athlete can transcend sports to become a force for good in the broader world. The skinny boy who threw rocks into the Caribbean Sea became a man who used his platform to serve others until his final day.

Fifty years after his passing, stadiums throughout Latin America and the United States bear his name. The right field wall at Pittsburgh's PNC Park remains 21 feet high in tribute to his uniform number. His bronze statue outside the stadium is inscribed with his most famous quote: "Any time you have an opportunity to make a difference in this world and you don't, then you are wasting your time on Earth."

The boy from Carolina who became The Great One—El Grande—left behind a legacy that continues to inspire both on and off the diamond. Roberto Clemente's story reminds us that a baseball player can be more than a sports hero; he can be a humanitarian hero whose impact outlives even his most spectacular plays.

As baseball historian David Maraniss wrote: "Roberto Clemente played baseball with furious grace, but what distinguished him above all was a sense of higher purpose and moral obligation that transcended the game."

Derek Jeter: The Captain Who Redefined Modern Leadership

On a crisp October night in the Bronx in 2001, with New York City still reeling from the September 11 terrorist attacks, a 27-year-old shortstop stepped to the plate in the 10th inning of World Series Game 4. The Yankees trailed the series 2-1 to the Arizona Diamondbacks, and the scoreboard showed a 3-3 tie as the clock struck midnight, pushing the game into November for the first time in World Series history.

What happened next would add another chapter to a career already filled with moments that seemed scripted for baseball immortality.

Derek Sanderson Jeter connected with Byung-Hyun Kim's pitch, sending a low line drive toward right field. As the ball cleared the wall by mere inches and fans erupted in celebration of the walk-off home run, broadcaster Michael Kay delivered a call that captured not just the moment but the player: "Derek Jeter has added another incredible chapter to the legend of the New York Yankees."

This "Mr. November" moment typified Jeter's uncanny ability to deliver in the most pressure-filled situations. Yet the foundation of Jeter's legendary status wasn't built on dramatic home runs—it was constructed through consistent excellence, unwavering leadership, and a deep understanding that how he played the game was as important as what he achieved.

Born on June 26, 1974, in Pequannock Township, New Jersey, Jeter's early life provided perfect preparation for his future role as the face of baseball's most storied franchise. His father, Charles, was African American and worked as a substance abuse counselor. His mother, Dorothy, was of Irish descent and worked as an accountant. The family moved to Kalamazoo, Michigan, when Derek was four, seeking better schools and opportunities.

From his earliest years, Jeter benefited from parents who combined high expectations with unwavering support. They established a "contract" with young Derek and his sister Sharlee, outlining academic and behavioral standards. This structure instilled both discipline and accountability—qualities that would define Jeter's professional approach.

"My parents always told me I could do anything I wanted to do, but I had to work for it," Jeter later recalled. "Nothing in life is handed to you. You have to earn everything you get."

Baseball became Derek's passion early. During summers, he would visit his grandparents in New Jersey, where he developed his love for the Yankees, particularly shortstop Dave Winfield. By high school, Jeter's talent was unmistakable. At Kalamazoo Central High School, he hit .508 as a junior and .508 again as a senior, striking out only once in his final two seasons. Major league scouts became regular attendees at his games.

The Yankees selected Jeter with the sixth overall pick in the 1992 MLB draft. Though other teams had concerns about Jeter's ability to remain at shortstop due to his 6'3" frame, Yankees scout Dick Groch famously told his superiors: "The only place this kid's going is to Cooperstown."

Jeter's minor league journey wasn't without challenges. In 1993, playing for the Class-A Greensboro Hornets, he committed a staggering 56 errors and struggled mentally with his defensive issues. Rather than becoming discouraged, Jeter worked tirelessly to improve, spending extra hours on fielding drills and learning to position himself better.

"I think the biggest thing I learned that season was how to deal with failure," Jeter later said. "You're going to fail in baseball. The important thing is how you respond to it."

This resilience would become a hallmark of Jeter's career. By 1995, he had worked his way to a brief 15-game major league debut with the Yankees. The following spring, veteran shortstop Tony Fernandez suffered an injury, creating an unexpected opportunity. Yankees manager Joe Torre, impressed with Jeter's maturity, named the 21-year-old his starting shortstop for Opening Day 1996.

Jeter's rookie season exceeded all expectations. He hit .314, scored 104 runs, and helped the Yankees win their first World Series since 1978. In Game 1 of that World Series against the Atlanta Braves, Jeter hit a controversial home run when 12-year-old fan Jeffrey Maier reached over the right field wall and interfered with the ball—an early glimpse of the seemingly charmed baseball life that would follow Jeter.

His rookie performance earned him the American League Rookie of the Year award, but more importantly, it established him as a cornerstone of what would become one of baseball's great dynasties. The Yankees would win three more World Series titles in the next four years (1998, 1999, 2000), with Jeter playing a central role in each championship.

What made Jeter exceptional wasn't just his statistical production, which was consistently excellent—he would finish his career with 3,465 hits, the sixth-highest total in MLB history—but the intangibles he brought to the

Yankees. His approach to the game combined old-school values with modern athletic brilliance.

Yankees teammate David Cone observed: "Derek has the perfect temperament for New York and for the position he plays. He never gets too high, never gets too low."

This even-keeled demeanor proved crucial in the pressure cooker of New York, where media scrutiny and fan expectations can overwhelm even the most talented players. Throughout his 20-year career, Jeter managed to maintain both his privacy and his reputation—a remarkable achievement in the tabloid capital of America.

On the field, certain moments and plays came to define the Jeter mystique. In the 2001 American League Division Series against Oakland, with the Yankees facing elimination, Jeter made his famous "flip play"—racing across the infield to retrieve an errant relay throw and flipping it to catcher Jorge Posada to tag out Jeremy Giambi at home plate. The improbable assist saved a run and helped the Yankees rally to win the series.

In a 2004 game against the Boston Red Sox, Jeter charged full speed after a foul popup and dove headlong into the stands, emerging with the ball and a bloodied face. The play exemplified his all-out approach and willingness to sacrifice his body.

"I only know one way to play," Jeter explained. "I give everything I have every time I step on the field."

In 2003, following the departure of veteran pitcher Roger Clemens, Yankees owner George Steinbrenner officially named Jeter the team captain—the first person to hold that title since Don Mattingly retired in 1995. The role formalized what had already become evident: Jeter was the team's unquestioned leader, setting standards through both his play and his professionalism.

As captain, Jeter led more by example than with fiery speeches. Teammates noted how he was always the first to arrive for workouts, his preparation was meticulous, and his focus unwavering. He established a culture where accountability and winning took precedence over individual achievements.

"There may be people with more talent than you," Jeter often said, "but there's no excuse for anyone to work harder than you."

This approach particularly resonated with younger players who joined the Yankees. Robinson Canó, who debuted with the team in 2005, later reflected: "Derek taught me that being a professional isn't just about what you do during the game. It's about how you prepare, how you carry yourself, how you treat people."

Jeter's leadership philosophy extended beyond the clubhouse. In 1996, he established the Turn 2 Foundation, focused on helping young people avoid drug and alcohol addiction through programs promoting healthy lifestyles. The name referenced both the baseball term for a double play and the idea of giving young people a "turn to" a better path.

This commitment to community service reflected Jeter's understanding that his influence extended beyond baseball. Though intensely private about his personal life, he recognized his responsibility as a role model, particularly for biracial children who saw themselves reflected in his success.

"I always wanted to be a Yankee," Jeter once said. "I was conscious of my color, but I never looked at myself as being a minority. I just looked at myself as a baseball player who wanted to be the best."

Jeter's career wasn't without challenges. In 2003, his previously close relationship with Yankees owner George Steinbrenner became strained during contentious contract negotiations, when Steinbrenner publicly questioned Jeter's commitment and leadership. Rather than responding defensively, Jeter simply continued to perform at a high level, letting his play answer the criticism.

A more serious test came in 2010 when, at age 36, Jeter experienced his worst statistical season, hitting just .270. Media narratives suggested his career was in decline, and subsequent contract negotiations with the Yankees proved difficult. The man who had represented the franchise with such distinction found himself in the awkward position of having to prove his worth.

"I'd be lying if I said I wasn't angry," Jeter admitted regarding the negotiations. But rather than taking his talents elsewhere, he returned to the Yankees on a new contract and responded with a stellar 2011 season, becoming just the 28th player in MLB history to reach 3,000 hits. Fittingly, he achieved the milestone with a home run, going 5-for-5 that day against the Tampa Bay Rays.

As his career entered its final phase, injuries became a significant challenge. A broken ankle in the 2012 American League Championship Series required surgery and limited him to just 17 games in 2013. Many questioned whether Jeter could return to form for his age-40 season in 2014.

In February 2014, Jeter announced on Facebook that the upcoming season would be his last. "I could not be more sure," he wrote. "I know it in my heart. The 2014 season will be my last year playing professional baseball."

What followed was an unprecedented farewell tour, with teams across the league honoring Jeter during his final visit to their stadiums. Some critics found the extended celebration excessive, but it reflected Jeter's unique status in the sport—respected even by the Yankees' fiercest rivals for how he played the game.

The final home game of Jeter's career on September 25, 2014, provided one last magical moment. With the score tied in the bottom of the ninth inning, Jeter delivered a walk-off single to right field in his final Yankee Stadium at-bat. As teammates mobbed him and fans chanted his name, the normally stoic Jeter fought back tears, later admitting: "I don't think I could have written it any better than this."

Three days later in Boston, Jeter collected his final hit, an RBI single, before being removed from the game to a standing ovation from the Fenway Park crowd—remarkable recognition from fans of the Yankees' greatest rival.

Jeter's final career statistics place him among baseball's elite: 3,465 hits (sixth all-time), 1,923 runs scored, 260 home runs, 358 stolen bases, and a career .310 batting average. His postseason numbers further burnish his legacy: 200 hits, 111 runs, 20 home runs, and a .308 batting average across 158 playoff games—essentially an additional full season performed under maximum pressure.

Beyond the numbers, Jeter's career is defined by consistency, durability, and winning. His teams made the playoffs in 16 of his 20 seasons. He won five World Series rings. He was selected to 14 All-Star teams and won five Gold Glove awards.

In retirement, Jeter has continued to demonstrate his leadership qualities. He became part-owner and CEO of the Miami Marlins from 2017 to 2022, making him the first Black person to hold such a position in MLB history. He was elected to the Baseball Hall of Fame in 2020, receiving 99.7% of the vote—the second-highest percentage ever at that time.

For young baseball players, Jeter's journey offers invaluable lessons that extend far beyond technique or statistics. His career demonstrates the importance of consistency and reliability—showing up every day ready to perform, regardless of circumstances. His approach to leadership illustrates how actions often speak louder than words, and how maintaining composure under pressure creates confidence throughout a team.

Perhaps most significantly, Jeter's career offers a template for handling fame and success with grace. In an era of expanding media coverage and social media scrutiny, he maintained both his privacy and his reputation through discipline and focus on what mattered most.

"My office is at Yankee Stadium," he once explained. "Yes, the pay is good, but I would do it for nothing."

That simple statement captures the essence of what made Derek Jeter special—a genuine love for baseball combined with an unwavering commitment to excellence. From that contract his parents made him sign as a child to his final moments on the field, Derek Jeter understood that greatness isn't granted; it's earned through daily choices and consistent effort.

The skinny kid from Kalamazoo who dreamed of playing shortstop for the Yankees didn't just achieve his childhood ambition—he redefined what a modern baseball leader could be. In a sport obsessed with statistics and measurables, Jeter reminded us that some of the most valuable contributions can't be quantified: integrity, composure under pressure, and the ability to elevate those around you.

As Jeter himself said in his Hall of Fame induction speech: "It's not the championships that drive me, or the records. It's having respect for the game, respect for the organization, respect for the uniform, respect for my teammates and my peers, and most importantly, the fans."

In the end, The Captain's legacy isn't just the championships or the highlight-reel plays—it's the standard of excellence and professionalism he established, a standard that will inspire generations of players to come.

Ken Griffey Jr.: The Natural Who Brought Joy Back to Baseball

On April 10, 1989, a lanky 19-year-old rookie with an infectious smile stepped into the batter's box at the Seattle Kingdome. With an easy, fluid swing that seemed almost effortless, he launched a pitch against the wall for a double in his first major league at-bat. Few could have imagined that this moment would launch not just a Hall of Fame career, but a cultural phenomenon that would help revitalize America's pastime during one of its darkest periods.

George Kenneth Griffey Jr.—known to millions simply as "The Kid"—would go on to redefine what was possible on a baseball field while reconnecting the sport with a younger generation through his electrifying play and genuine joy.

Born in Donora, Pennsylvania, on November 21, 1969—exactly 49 years to the day after baseball legend Stan Musial was born in the same small town—Griffey seemed destined for baseball greatness. His father, Ken Griffey Sr., was already establishing himself as an All-Star outfielder with the Cincinnati Reds' "Big Red Machine" dynasty.

Growing up in a major league clubhouse provided Junior with an extraordinary baseball education. As a child, he observed stars like Johnny Bench, Joe Morgan, and Pete Rose up close, absorbing their techniques and approaches to the game. He shagged fly balls during batting practice and received hitting tips from some of the game's greatest minds.

But this privileged access to baseball excellence came with challenges. Being the son of a major leaguer created enormous expectations and intense scrutiny. Some assumed any success would be the product of nepotism rather than talent. Others expected him to be as good as his father immediately.

"People always compared me to my dad," Griffey later recalled. "That was tough sometimes because he was an established big leaguer, and I was just a kid trying to figure things out."

The family moved to Cincinnati when Ken Sr. joined the Reds, and it was at Archbishop Moeller High School where Junior's exceptional talent became evident. His high school coach Mike Cameron remembered: "Ken was the best player I've ever coached. He had all five tools at an advanced level even as a teenager."

Professional scouts agreed. The Seattle Mariners selected Griffey with the first overall pick in the 1987 MLB draft, beginning an unlikely relationship between a transcendent talent and a struggling franchise that had never experienced a winning season.

After less than two years in the minor leagues, Griffey forced his way onto the Mariners' 1989 Opening Day roster through his outstanding spring training performance. At 19, he became the youngest player in the major leagues, but his youth didn't translate to struggles. He hit .264 with 16 home runs in his rookie season, displaying flashes of the all-around brilliance that would soon make him baseball's most exciting player.

What made Griffey special wasn't just his statistical production but how he achieved it. His left-handed swing was poetry in motion—a perfect balance of technical precision and natural grace that coaches still use as a model for young hitters. His defensive abilities were equally spectacular, featuring full-extension diving catches and leaps above the outfield wall to rob home runs.

"The thing about Junior was that he made the extraordinary seem routine," said former teammate Jay Buhner. "He'd make a play that should have been on highlight reels for weeks, and he'd just jog back to the dugout with that smile like it was no big deal."

That smile became Griffey's trademark—a genuine expression of the joy he found in playing baseball. While many players approached the game with stern intensity, Griffey reminded everyone that baseball was, at its core, a game meant to be enjoyed. He played with his cap turned backward during batting practice and home run derbies, a small act of individuality that connected with young fans but occasionally irritated baseball traditionalists.

By his third season, Griffey had blossomed into a superstar, hitting .327 with 22 home runs and winning his first Gold Glove award. The following year, 1991, he made the first of what would become 13 All-Star appearances. In 1993, he truly arrived as one of baseball's elite players, hitting 45 home runs, driving in 109 runs, and leading the American League in total bases while continuing to provide Gold Glove defense in center field.

Perhaps the most emotional moment of Griffey's early career came in 1990 when the Seattle Mariners signed Ken Griffey Sr., creating the first father-son teammate combination in MLB history. On September 14, 1990, they made history again by hitting back-to-back home runs against the California Angels—an unprecedented family achievement that generated national attention.

"That was the highlight of my career," Junior later said. "Not the All-Star Games or the Gold Gloves, but playing alongside my dad. How many people get to go to work with their father and do something they both love?"

As Griffey's star rose, he faced a decision that would define his career and legacy. After the 1995 season, as he approached the prime of his career and free agency loomed, many expected him to leave Seattle for a larger market and bigger contract. Instead, he signed a four-year, $34 million extension with the Mariners—at the time, the largest contract in baseball history, but almost certainly less than he could have commanded on the open market.

Griffey's commitment to Seattle was rewarded in 1995 with one of the most magical seasons in franchise history. With the Mariners at risk of being relocated due to an aging stadium and financial struggles, the team made an improbable late-season comeback to win the AL West and reach the playoffs for the first time. In the decisive Game 5 of the Division Series against the New York Yankees, Griffey scored the winning run, sprinting from first base on Edgar Martinez's double and sliding home with a smile that became the defining image of Seattle baseball.

That playoff run, led by Griffey, saved baseball in Seattle. It generated the community support necessary to approve construction of a new stadium (now T-Mobile Park) and secured the franchise's future in the Pacific Northwest.

From 1996 to 1999, Griffey entered the stratosphere of baseball greatness. During this four-year stretch, he averaged 52 home runs and 142 RBIs per season, won four consecutive Gold Gloves, and finished in the top five of MVP voting each year, winning the award in 1997.

His 1997 MVP season was a masterpiece: 56 home runs, 147 RBIs, 125 runs scored, and a .304 batting average, combined with his customary defensive excellence. In an era before advanced analytics, Griffey passed both the statistical test and the "eye test" with flying colors. There was little debate that he was baseball's most complete player.

Beyond his on-field achievements, Griffey's cultural impact was immeasurable. He starred in commercials for Nike, appeared on the cover of Nintendo's Ken Griffey Jr. Presents Major League Baseball video game, and even received a cameo role in The Simpsons. His backward cap became a fashion statement for an entire generation of young baseball fans. His Nike signature cleats were among the most popular in baseball.

Critically, Griffey achieved this popularity while maintaining a clean image and strong values. In an era when baseball would soon be tarnished by performance-enhancing drug scandals, Griffey's achievements came without such asterisks. He was a family man who prioritized being present for his children, sometimes bringing his son Trey into the clubhouse just as his father had done with him.

Following the 1999 season, Griffey requested a trade to Cincinnati to be closer to his family, who lived there during the offseason. The Mariners respected his wishes, trading him to the Reds in February 2000 for a package of players. Griffey then signed a nine-year, $116.5 million contract with Cincinnati—again, significantly less than he could have commanded on the open market, a decision made to help the Reds build a competitive team around him.

The Cincinnati chapter of Griffey's career proved bittersweet. While he continued to produce when healthy—hitting his 500th and 600th career home runs in a Reds uniform—a series of injuries prevented him from maintaining the consistent excellence he had shown in Seattle. Hamstring injuries, a torn knee tendon, and broken bones diminished his once-supernatural athleticism.

"The hardest part was knowing what I was capable of doing and not being able to do it anymore," Griffey later reflected. "I knew what my body was supposed to do, but it wouldn't respond the way it once did."

Despite these physical challenges, Griffey persevered, adapting his game and continuing to produce. Even in his diminished physical state, he hit 35 home runs in 2005 at age 35 and remained a positive clubhouse influence for younger players.

After brief stints with the Chicago White Sox and a return to Seattle for his final season and a half, Griffey retired in June 2010 with 630 career home runs (seventh all-time), 1,836 RBIs (15th), 2,781 hits, and 10 Gold Gloves. His WAR (Wins Above Replacement) of 83.8 ranks 35th in MLB history, with his peak seasons ranking even higher.

In 2016, Griffey was elected to the Baseball Hall of Fame with 99.32% of the vote—at that time, the highest percentage ever, a fitting recognition of both his statistical achievements and his importance to the sport. True to form, he wore his cap backward during his Hall of Fame induction speech.

Beyond the numbers, Griffey's legacy lies in how he changed baseball's culture and appeal. He arrived at a time when baseball was perceived as stodgy and traditional compared to the more dynamic NBA and NFL. His combination of extraordinary talent and genuine enthusiasm helped reconnect the sport with younger fans.

"What I remember most isn't any particular hit or catch," said former Mariners manager Lou Piniella. "It's how much pure joy Ken brought to the ballpark every day. When he smiled, everyone smiled with him."

For young baseball players, Griffey's career offers several important lessons. His natural talent was undeniable, but he combined it with a tireless work ethic, particularly on defense. Despite his early success, he continued refining his skills throughout his career. When injuries limited his physical tools later in his career, he adjusted his approach rather than giving up.

Perhaps most importantly, Griffey demonstrated that excellence doesn't require sacrificing joy. In a sport where players often adopt stoic personas, he showed that enthusiasm and fun are compatible with the highest levels of achievement.

"I played the game how I wanted to play it," Griffey explained in his Hall of Fame speech. "I tried to catch every ball hit in my direction. I tried to throw out every runner. I tried to make every play. I played the game with excitement, passion and a lot of determination."

The skinny teenager who entered the Kingdome with a backward cap and a megawatt smile grew into a legend who helped save a franchise and rejuvenate a sport. Ken Griffey Jr.'s legacy isn't just in the record books or on highlight reels—it's in how he reminded baseball and its fans that extraordinary achievement and genuine joy can go hand in hand.

As former commissioner Bud Selig observed: "In an era that produced so many great players, Ken stood out not just for what he accomplished but for how he accomplished it. He played the game with a combination of grace, power, and joy that inspired an entire generation."

From father-son home runs to leaping catches above the outfield wall, from that picture-perfect swing to the radiant smile that followed, The Kid showed us all what baseball at its very best could be—a perfect blend of excellence and exuberance that reminded us why we fell in love with the game in the first place.

Chapter 13
Baseball Star Glossary

At-bat: When a player takes their turn batting against the pitcher.

Backstop: The fence or wall behind home plate that stops wild pitches and foul balls.

Balk: An illegal motion by the pitcher that results in baserunners advancing one base.

Batting average: A statistic that measures a batter's success by dividing hits by at-bats.

Bullpen: The area where pitchers warm up before entering the game.

Bunt: A batting technique where the batter holds the bat in the path of the ball without swinging, causing the ball to roll slowly into the infield.

Change-up: A slow pitch thrown with the same arm motion as a fastball to deceive the batter.

Crossover step: The first movement a baserunner makes when starting to run, crossing one foot over the other.

Crow hop: A technique used by outfielders to generate momentum for a throw by taking a small hop before throwing.

Curveball: A breaking pitch that curves or drops as it approaches the batter.

Cutoff man: An infielder who positions themselves between an outfielder and the intended base to relay throws.

Dugout: The area along the first and third base lines where team members sit when not on the field.

Double play: A defensive play where two offensive players are put out on the same play.

Fastball: A straight pitch thrown at maximum speed.

Fielder's choice: When a fielder chooses to put out another runner instead of the batter running to first base.

Ground ball: A batted ball that rolls or bounces on the ground.

Hidden ball trick: A play where an infielder pretends to throw the ball back to the pitcher but actually keeps it to tag a runner who steps off base.

Home run: A hit that allows the batter to circle all the bases and score, typically by hitting the ball over the outfield fence.

Hook slide: A sliding technique where the runner hooks their foot around the base while sliding to avoid a tag.

Infield: The area inside the bases, where the infielders play.

Inning: A division of the game consisting of a turn at bat for each team.

Lead: The distance a baserunner takes off a base before the pitcher delivers the ball.

Line drive: A hard-hit ball that travels in a straight line without much arc.

MLB: Major League Baseball, the highest level of professional baseball.

On deck: The batter scheduled to bat after the current batter.

Outfield: The grassy area beyond the infield where outfielders play.

Pickoff move: An attempt by the pitcher to throw out a runner leading off base.

Pop fly (or Pop-up): A ball hit high into the air that stays in the infield.

Pop-up slide: A slide that ends with the runner standing up, ready to advance to the next base if possible.

Rally: When a team scores multiple runs in a single inning, especially when coming from behind.

RBI (Run Batted In): A statistic credited to a batter whose action results in a run being scored.

Rundown: When a baserunner is caught between two bases with fielders trying to tag them out.

Sacrifice fly: A fly ball that allows a runner to tag up and score after it's caught.

Situational hitting: Batting with a specific goal based on the game situation (like advancing a runner).

Slider: A breaking pitch that moves laterally and down as it reaches the batter.

Squeeze play: When a runner on third base runs home as the batter bunts.

Strike zone: The area over home plate between the batter's knees and mid-chest where pitches count as strikes.

Submarine style: A pitching technique where the ball is thrown with an underhand motion.

Tag up: When a runner waits on their base until a fly ball is caught, then attempts to advancc.

Warning track: The dirt path that runs along the outfield wall, warning fielders they're approaching the wall.

Wild pitch: An errant pitch that the catcher cannot catch, allowing runners to advance.

Made in United States
Orlando, FL
09 June 2025